The Inadvertent Epic
From Uncle Tom's Cabin to Roots

Leslie A. Fiedler

Samuel Clemens Professor of English
State University of New York at Buffalo

With an Introduction by
Barrie Hayne
Associate Professor of English and Film
Innis College, University of Toronto

A Touchstone Book
Published by Simon and Schuster
New York

Previously published by *CBC Merchandising* for the Canadian Broadcasting Corporation.

Manufactured in the United States of America

1   2   3   4   5   6   7   8   9   10   Pbk.

Library of Congress Cataloging in Publication Data

Fiedler, Leslie A.
  The inadvertent epic.

  (A Touchstone book)
    1.   American fiction—History and criticism.
2.   Epic literature, American—History and criticism.
3.   Popular literature—United States—History and criticism.   I.   Title.
PS371.F54   813'.03   79-26481

ISBN 0-671-25372-7 Pbk.

The Inadvertent Epic is based on a five-part radio broadcast of the 1978 Massey Lectures which were aired in October of that year as part of CBC's IDEAS series. The programs were produced by Geraldine Sherman, executive producer of IDEAS. The Massey Lectures were created in honour of the Right Honourable Vincent Massey, former Governor General of Canada, and were inaugurated by the CBC in 1961 to enable distinguished authorities to present the results of original study or research on a variety of subjects of general interest.

Contents

Introduction

"I like disturbing the peace, wherever that peace seems to
me the product not of mediation but of torpor and fear"

In the autobiography he wrote in 1969, *Being Busted*, and
elsewhere, Leslie Fiedler has objected to being called "controversial," but it seems to be a word which the writers of
dust jacket blurbs—and introductions—cannot do without in
discussing him. Yet to call Fiedler controversial, as in particular so many of his fellow academics in the last thirty years
have done, is to draw attention to one's own failure to recognize the true (even the obvious) function of criticism, and the
academy—which is to controvert the easily accepted, to disturb the sleep of a decided opinion.

To those, nonetheless, who are content to leave conventional wisdom in its wonted slumber, Fiedler has long been
an irritant. To his fellow Marxists, or even his fellow liberals,
it is plainly unacceptable to call Alger Hiss a perjurer, or to
see the Rosenbergs guilty as charged. To many Jews it is no
less objectionable to raise the spectre of black anti-semitism
(or its opposite). And to his fellow critics of American literature, some few of whom might like to remember *Moby-Dick*,
Huckleberry Finn and the novels of James Fenimore Cooper
as children's books, and many more of whom prefer to analyze
such works according to the canons of High Art only, it is
disagreeable to find them thrust forward as embodying the
fascinating taboos of homosexuality and miscegenation so
deeply repressed in the national psyche. *Love and Death in
the American Novel*, in 1960, as much a revolutionary work
of definition for our century as Fiedler himself gives *American
Renaissance* credit for being, forced the academy to see those

very taboos and myths writ on a much larger and more extensive scale, across the whole range of American fiction. *The Inadvertent Epic* will, no less, disturb the slumber of academic opinion. It is, in fact, the obverse of *Love and Death*.

The earlier work (to which must be added the "sequels" of *The Return of the Vanishing American* and *Waiting for the End*, and the great preliminary essay "Come Back to the Raft Ag'in, Huck Honey,") defined a dominant theme, in the classic American novel, of male bonding, of "homosexual" antipathy for a society pervasively seen as under the sway of women, matriarchal. *The Inadvertent Epic* turns away from these classics, taught in any academic classroom, to scrutinize instead a tradition of works (*Uncle Tom's Cabin*, *The Clansman*, *The Birth of a Nation*, *Gone With the Wind*, *Roots*) which rarely find a place in the classroom, and which embody not a male, subversive, anti-family myth, but a feminine, pro-society, domestic and familial one, but which are just as potent, and, in their grasp on a wider popular imagination, probably even more so.

In the process of defining this other side of the male bonding theme, of course, Fiedler puts us in possession of nothing less than a new method of approaching literature itself. If such enormously potent works as *Uncle Tom's Cabin* and *Gone With the Wind*, known, at least in some of their elements, to almost everybody on the globe, fall short when measured by academic literary standards, by the canons of High Art, then let us re-examine those standards and canons to see whether they, not the potent objects of their judgment, may be at fault. Out of this inquiry comes the approach to literature as popular culture—though it is well to remember that we ought to arrive at *Gone With the Wind* from the classics rather than starting from it, as the anecdote of the girl from Sacred Heart Academy makes clear.

One of the "books" of Fiedler's inadvertent epic, *The Birth of a Nation*, seems at first glance to fit uncomfortably into the design. While it is certainly based on one part of the continuing epic which is itself a refutation of the first part, Griffith's film differs from the other parts in that it is a work technically superior, thematically conscious, the work of an artist. But even here Fiedler's point is finally incontrovertible, for what is stamped on the popular imagination from *The Birth of a Nation* is less its artistic virtuosity than its embodiment of a myth, and its transcendence, as Fiedler says of *Uncle Tom*, of not only criteria of taste, but credibility itself. It is difficult to quarrel with Fiedler's distillation of the essence of this great film with such precision, into that single memorable image of the Klan riding to the rescue, of "those silent hooves pounding as if forever through a dream landscape."

It is, indeed, "dream" that has so often engaged Fiedler's attention—the intangible, often unconsciously conveyed, as unconsciously received, content of the work of art, or sub-art, which takes it far beyond its literal meaning to "the realer-than-real vividness of hallucinations." As a university teacher he writes movingly (and here, as elsewhere, disarmingly, in his confessions of academic ambivalence towards *Gone With the Wind* or the soaps), and as a university teacher he has written, during the turbulent '60s, of the idea and role of a university. To him it is neither the ivory tower of the pre-1960s, nor the slave of "public relations," having "public service of some kind" as its *primary* obligation. It also seeks access to the "dream": "the primary purpose of a university should be not to serve things-as-they-are, the oppressive present, but to provide a refuge from its exigencies in the study of an alien past, and to suggest alternatives to it by foreshadowing an alien future. The dream of that past and the dream of that future—for future and past are dreams or they are nothing—the university must not merely teach but live, . . . a model of the permanent and inalienable freedom to be something else, rather than an example of subservience to the demands of whatever group happens to possess power at any given moment." If more people listened to these words, even (or especially) today, the universities and the societies which surround them would be in less trouble than they are.

What Leslie Fiedler is doing in *The Inadvertent Epic* (a title richly suggestive of the gap between narrow intention and transcendent achievement, itself a tapping of dream) is continuing what he has always done—interpreting the United States and its culture to itself and to outsiders. The American "Dream," in some writers a debased cliche, has meaning for him, a meaning of stretching beyond one's limitations, as *Uncle Tom's Cabin* stretches beyond its conventional limitations. He has written of the necessity not of *being* an American, but of *keeping on becoming one:* the necessity of constant redefinition "to suit oneself, one's history, and one's fate." He has sought such self-definition in a great variety of foreign forums, Toronto among them, but in three principal American places: in his native Newark, the epitome of urban America; in Missoula, Montana, close to the Indian America, where he lived and taught for twenty years; and now for the past fifteen years in Buffalo, "an *ex-*Western city," eastern, yet on the Niagara "Frontier." His saturation in Mark Twain (who also lived briefly in Buffalo), his fascination with the frontier, along with his late-Twainian sense of its disappearance, hinted at even in his titles (*An End to Innocence, The Last Jew in America, Waiting for the End*), his somewhat naif (though hardly unsophisticated) exuberance in life, his occasional sense of being society's victim ("to take on the role that Sacco and Vanzetti had accepted . . . but Alger Hiss and Julius Rosenberg had refused") even his present position as Samuel Clemens Professor at SUNY—these qualities give Fiedler finally the appearance of what a highly articulate and intelligent Huck Finn might have become had we followed his career into its fifth or sixth decades, and had he been miraculously transported into our own more-than-the-Gilded-Age chaotic world. Fiedler's self-evoked sense of victimization has enabled him, no doubt, to write so sympathetically of the black American, and the Red; and certainly no one has written so well or so clear-headedly of the American Jew —especially in the collection *To the Gentiles* (the characteristic sense of mission is there in the title) or in the novel *The Last Jew in America,* where his sympathetic irony saves him from the self-pity of a Malamud or the callousness of a Philip Roth. But what strikes one as one surveys Fiedler's achievement as a writer on American themes (themes to which, as a student of Shakespeare and Dante, he is by no means confined) is the very range: from Huck and McCarthy in the 50s to Chang and Eng and Alex Haley twenty and thirty years later.

The grand truth about Nathaniel Hawthorne, as Melville (clearly thinking more of himself) remarked, was that he said "No! in thunder; but the Devil himself cannot make him say *yes.''* The grand truth about Leslie Fiedler (who borrowed Melville's phrase for the title of his second collection of essays) is that, yes, he does say No! in thunder, but that more often than not the no is ultimately a way of saying yes; the whole direction of his career is towards affirmation. When in 1970 he wrote a new preface for *No! In Thunder*, he noted that it had taken him ''a long time to realize that the obligation to praise does not contradict but complements the necessity to say no.'' Yet this is surely a realization he has always had, for in the preface to the first edition he had written, in reference to Faulkner: ''In the end, the negativist is no nihilist, for he affirms the void.'' ''He chooses, rather, to render the absurdity which he perceives, to know it and make it known.'' This continues to be Fiedler's mission, and he has continued to convey that mission as a ''dream,'' quixotic though it may sometimes be. Call him Freudian, Jungian, archetypal, mythic, cultural, critic (all these terms have their limitations), he is projecting the cultural dreams and bringing his readers into contact with them. To be asked to look at one's comfortable assumptions, especially as they concern self and country, is painful enough; to be confronted with one's national and personal dreams, the repressed products of one's hidden recesses, is infinitely more painful. Which is why some regard him as ''controversial.'' But health and self-understanding lie in the direction Fiedler is pointing.

Barrie Hayne

1 *Uncle Tom's Cabin:* The Invisible Masterpiece

Of all American novels, surely the most widely read and deeply loved—not just in the country of its origin, but throughout the world—is *Uncle Tom's Cabin*. Yet most elitist critics have found it an artistic failure, ill-constructed, shamefully sentimental and annoyingly shrill, its characters stereotypes, its plot vulgar melodrama. No wonder that the guardians of high taste, embarrassed by its unwillingness to go away and die the death to which it has been repeatedly condemned, have chosen to pretend it is no longer there. In F.O. Matthiessen's *American Renaissance*, for instance, which established for our century a new canon of mid-nineteenth century literature, Mrs. Stowe is accorded only a few passing words; and earlier, D.H. Lawrence had ignored her completely in his equally influential *Studies in Classic American Literature*: a book in which he manages to define what he calls "the Spirit of Place" without alluding to any American book by a woman or about a Negro.

The compilers of handbooks for classroom use are forced to acknowledge at least the existence of a work which has pleased so many for so long; but they tend to apologize for doing so. *The Literary History of the United States*, for instance, concludes a little mournfully that "Harriet Beecher Stowe was neither a great personality nor a great artist...", while the editors of a recent college anthology preface their selection from her improbable masterpiece by asking themselves, "How good is *Uncle Tom's Cabin* as a novel?", and answering, "Not very good if we judge it by the highest fictional standards." Once the words "great" and "highest" have been invoked, one knows the verdict will go against the book which Mrs. Stowe liked to boast (in what seems the last refuge of an inept author) had been really written by God.

In any case, by 1960 when my own *Love and Death in the American Novel* appeared, *Uncle Tom's Cabin* had come to seem a nearly invisible work, the "nigger" of American literature. To be sure, it has had its defenders, from Tolstoi to V.L. Parrington and Van Wyck Brooks, all of them apologists for some "higher cause," in whose name they were willing to permit her what they agree are egregious artistic faults. "Despite its obvious blemishes of structure and sentimentalism," Parrington writes, for instance, "it is a great human document...it was noble propaganda..." But the book in all its hallucinatory specificity tends to disappear from his favorable account even as it does from the blanket condemnations of the formalist critics. So that I felt myself to be engaging in a task nearly heroic, certainly unprecedented, when in *Love and Death* I tried to reconstruct *Uncle Tom's Cabin* (a book which, after all, I have read ten or twelve times, never without tears, since acquiring my first copy at age seven) sympathetically and in detail. Finally, however, influenced by Matthiessen and Lawrence, I undercut my praise by observing that as a "genteel sentimentalist," Mrs. Stowe was incapable of "tragic ambivalence," a quality which, like those mentors, I then extravangantly prized.

I went on, moreover, to accuse her of being even less capable of "radical Protest"; since I had just read James Baldwin's essay "Everybody's Protest Novel," in which he condemned *Uncle Tom's Cabin* from the point of view both of an avant-garde aesthete and an embattled American Black, who found Mrs. Stowe's politics along with the ethnic myths which sustained it profoundly objectionable. *"Uncle Tom's Cabin,"* Baldwin the literary critic writes, "is a very bad novel, having in its self-righteous, virtuous sentimentality, much in common with *Little Women*. Sentimentality, the ostentatious parading of excessive and spurious emotion, is the mark of dishonesty, the inability to feel...and it is always, therefore, the signal of secret and violent inhumanity, the mask of cruelty..." Then he adds in a cry of masculine protest, "Tom...has been robbed of his humanity and divested of his sex." Yet Baldwin confesses elsewhere that Mrs. Stowe's novel had been one of his favorite boyhood books—describing how he simultaneously tended his younger brothers and sisters and redreamed her "excessive and spurious" dream of black martyrdom. "As they were born," he tells us, "I took them over with one hand and held a book in the other...and in this way I read *Uncle Tom's Cabin*... over and over and over again." But that early passion for her prose he later rejected entirely, and his total recantation helped persuade me to make my own partial one.

Measured by the standards of high literature, *Uncle Tom's Cabin* is a failure; of this there seems to me still no doubt; and in 1960 I could find no way out short of rejecting that book. But in the nearly two decades since, I have begun to reverse the process which led me into that trap, by measuring my inherited notions of appropriate criteria for literature against *Uncle Tom's Cabin*,

15

instead of it against them. It is not simply a matter of coming to terms with the popular adulation of *Uncle Tom's Cabin*, which I was taught all too easily to despise, but with my own instinctive responses, which I found it harder to learn to distrust; though learning that lesson, my teachers assured me, would distinguish me forever from the mass audience, imperfectly educated and largely female, which prefers the easy sentimentality of *Little Women, Uncle Tom's Cabin* and Daytime Serials on TV to the "tragic ambiguity" and "radical protest" of *Moby Dick* and *Leaves of Grass*. Yet, though I have for nearly half a century paid my professional respects to Melville and Whitman, I find myself weeping still over the deaths of Little Eva and Beth, and from time to time even sneak off to watch the Soaps.

I have determined, therefore, to deal head on with what I can only hypocritically disavow; and to save *Uncle Tom's Cabin*—even if this means re-defining literature as it has been traditionally understood, as well as reconstituting the canon of o.k. fiction as defined by *American Renaissance* and *Studies in Classic American Literature*. I propose, moreover, to redeem for serious literary discussion not just Mrs. Stowe's book and the "Tom Plays" into which it was translated, but certain other works descended from it and them, and even more despised by established critics: Thomas Dixon Jr.'s *The Leopard's Spots* and *The Clansman* (along with *The Birth of a Nation*, a film derived from them by D.W. Griffith), Margaret Mitchell's *Gone With the Wind* (both as a novel and a movie) and Alex Haley's *Roots* (in all of its pop avatars from predigested book selection to what promises to become an endless T.V. series).

Understood as a single work composed over more

than a century, in many media and by many hands, these constitute a hitherto unperceived Popular Epic. Rooted in demonic dreams of race, sex and violence which have long haunted us Americans, they determine our views of the Civil War, Reconstruction, the Rise and Fall of the Ku Klux Klan, the enslavement and liberation of African Blacks, thus constituting a myth of our history unequalled in scope or resonance by any work of High Literature.

No Epic, however, was ever created so inadvertently, so improbably, arising out of tradition at once disreputable and genteel, which seemed destined forever to produce not literature of high seriousness, "doctrinal to a nation," but only ephemeral best-sellers. Written in the nineteenth century chiefly by amateurs, clergymen and women (Harriet Beecher Stowe was not only a female amateur, but the daughter, wife and sister of clergymen), such best-sellers were accused by hightone critics and more pretentious novelists, competing for the mass audience, of contributing to the degradation of American culture. The books such writers preferred were not only more elegantly structured and textured, more ideologically dense, more overtly subversive— more difficult and challenging, in short; but, as it turned out, they almost invariably celebrated the flight from home and mother, civilization and the settlement, church and school, everything which survived (under female auspices) of Christian Humanism in the New World.

It is such works which are taught in school and preserved in libraries: "Rip Van Winkle," *The Last of the Mohicans, Moby-Dick, Huckleberry Finn, The Sun Also Rises, Henderson the Rain King.* And the mythos of

17

television shows such as *The Maltese Falcon, One Flew Over the Cuckoo's Nest, Starsky and Hutch, Star Trek.*

In the world of popular literature, however, a counter-tradition dominated by women and domestic values has also survived. Before our T.V. set, we continue to live with both; responding turn by turn to the rival myths they embody: the myth of the Family as Utopia and the Family as Dystopia, Home as Heaven and Home as Hell, Woman as Redeemer and Woman as Destroyer. Until dusk, our television screens are possessed by images of domesticity, acted out in closed rooms from which no one seems ever to escape: an environment sealed in by three walls of the set (the actual one behind us completes the closure), most often a home, inside of which no one is ever alone for more than a brief moment, since all the players aspire to and achieve (however briefly) heterosexual bonding, marriage and children. But once night falls, we are out on the streets again, under sail, riding the range, penetrating remotest space. And where permanent bonding occurs, it is likely to join two otherwise unattached males: Starsky and Hutch, Captain Kirk and Mr. Spock.

When we enter the classroom, however, or turn to the required reading lists, we discover only examples of the first, the male tradition, though both have, in fact, possessed our literature from its earliest beginnings. In fact, Richardsonian best-sellers like Susanna Rowson's *Charlotte Temple* delighted not just female readers but everyone, before male-oriented fantasies by Washington Irving, James Fenimore Cooper and Charles Brockden Brown had persuaded critics that the United States possessed a respectable literature of its own. And such books have continued to be produced for an undiminished audience by writers whom critics have refused to

18

recognize as full participants in that literature: Susan Warner, Mrs. E.D.E.N. Southworth, Louisa May Alcott, Helen Hunt Jackson, Fannie Hurst, Edna Ferber, Jacqueline Susann and Taylor Caldwell, to name only a few of the "horde of damned female scribblers" (the phrase is Hawthorne's) whom our literary establishment has found little difficulty in dismissing out of hand.

Only Harriet Beecher Stowe remains problematical—a contender for inclusion in a misogynist canon which begins with Washington Irving and extends to Saul Bellow ("What do they want?" he asks of women in *Herzog*. "They eat green salad and they drink blood.") Yet her values, like her tone, her style, her basic appeal, are those of the excluded female many rather than the chosen male few. In fact, at the heart of her housebound, mother centered novel, which begins and ends indoors—creating an astonishing gallery of homes ranging from Tom's humble cabin to the elegant Summer Cottage of the St. Clares—the myth of the Utopian Household receives its classic formulation. The Earthly Paradise which Mrs. Stowe describes is presumably an ordinary Quaker Household, maternal, nurturing, almost edible, and—be it noted—*all White* except for Eliza, a Black mother fleeing to save her child, and George, her bitter and troubled husband, who rejoins her there by happy chance.

The names of the inhabitants, however, are allegorical (the presiding matriarch is called, for instance, Rachel Halliday, in memory of the Old Testament Mother forever weeping for her children and refusing to be comforted); and the archetypal implications of the scene are reinforced by references to an Unfallen Eden in which an aging and chaste Venus peacefully reigns.

19

. . . all moved obediently to Rachel's gentle "Thee had better," or more gentle "Hadn't thee better?" on the work of getting breakfast; for a breakfast in the luxurious valleys of Indiana is a thing complicated and multiform, and like picking up the rose-leaves . . . in Paradise, asking other hands than those of the original mother . . . Bards have written of the cestus of Venus, that turned the heads of all the world in successive generations. We had rather, for our part, have the cestus of Rachel Halliday, that kept heads from being turned, and made everything go on harmoniously. We think it is more suited to our modern days, decidedly.

More resonant mythologically than the classical or Biblical names, however, are the words "mother" and "home" which echo and re-echo through the passage:

Rachel never looked so truly and benignly happy as at the head of her table. There was so much motherliness and full-heartedness even in the way she passed a plate of cakes or poured a cup of coffee, that it seemed to put a spirit into the food and drink she offered... This, indeed, was a home,—*home*,—...

It is, in fact, the assimilation of the Slavery Issue into so homely a scene which won the hearts of the readers of "female" best-sellers, ordinarily indifferent to the world of "male" politics; persuading them that the "patriarchal institution," as Mrs. Stowe typically called slavery, was a threat to the Home and Mother family. Once freed, she suggested, Black Americans would aspire to the kind of "Happy ending" which she and her genteel audience demanded of their favorite novels: the reunion of parents and children, husbands and wives in monogamous Christian households.

Just such a household she describes at the Dickens-like, tearful-cheerful conclusion of her book, when

George and Eliza, safe across the Canadian border, gather together not just with their son and daughter, but a miraculously preserved and re-discovered mother and sister, in a truly Pickwickian love-feast.

> The scene now changes to a small, neat tenement, in the outskirts of Montreal; the time, evening. A cheerful fire blazes on the hearth; a tea-table, covered with a snowy cloth, stands prepared for the evening meal... But to return to our friends, whom we left wiping their eyes, and recovering from too great and sudden a joy. They are now seated around the social board, and are getting decidedly companionable...

If George, the new head of his own house, dreams of a further emigration to Africa, it is not in order to "light out for the territory ahead of the rest," like Huckleberry Finn, to whom domestic "civilization" seems the end rather than the beginning of freedom; much less is it to search for his "roots," like some late twentieth century Black Nationalist. Far from desiring to find an alternative to the Christian Culture which has enslaved and un-manned him, a way of life based on polytheism, tribalism, polygamy or free sexuality, he plans to spread the Christian Gospel to his unredeemed brethren on the Dark Continent: "As a Christian patriot, a teacher of Christianity, I go to *my country*," he writes to a friend; and doubtless Mrs. Stowe's first fans dreamed of his bringing to the benighted not just literacy and "the sublime doctrine of love and forgiveness," but "small, neat tenements" and "snowy tablecloths" as well.

Not even those mothers, however, whom Mrs. Stowe continually addresses in asides ("If it were *your* Harry, mother, or your Will, that were going to be torn from you...tomorrow morning...") seem to have been much moved by the evocation of the servantless Quaker household, in which order is so effortlessly preserved and even the furniture is motherly; nor have the loving but desexed characters who inhabit it lived on among their dearest memories. What has continued to survive in the imagination not just of mothers but the whole world is what is truly mythic in *Uncle Tom's Cabin*.

In the Quaker Household, we are dealing not with myth but mythology—contrived, self-conscious, verging on allegory—a fantasy arising not out of the public nightmares of race and sex which Mrs. Stowe shared with her contemporaries in a nation moving toward total war, but out of her personal insecurities: her fear of growing old, her conviction that she was not beautiful, her inability to control her children (a favorite son would become an alcoholic and drift from sight) or to keep her house in order, though she in fact always had servants, some of them Black and all apparently as inefficient as she. Writing of a typical day in her own non-Utopian household, Mrs. Stowe walks the thin line between hilarity and despair.

This meal being cleared away, Mr. Stowe dispatched to market with various memoranda of provisions, etc., and baby being washed and dressed, I begin to think what next must be done. I start to cut out some little dresses...when Master Henry makes a doleful lip and falls to crying with might and main. I catch him up and, turning round, see one of his sisters flourishing the things out of my workbox in fine style. Moving it away and looking the other side, I see the second little mischief seated by the hearth chewing coals and scraping up ashes with great apparent relish. Grandmother lays hold upon her and charitably offers to endeavor to quiet baby while I go on with my work. I set at it again...pieces, measure them once more to see which is the right one, and proceed...when I see the twins on the point of quarreling with each other. Number one pushes number two over. Number two screams: that frightens baby, and he joins in. I call number one a naughty girl, take the persecuted one in my arms, and endeavor to comfort her...

How different the Hallidays, Rachel, her impotent and scarcely visible husband, her incredibly cheerful and cooperative children, are not just from Mrs. Stowe, her husband and their children, but even more from others of her characters, mysteriously known even to those who have never read Mrs. Stowe's novel: Uncle Tom, Eliza, Topsy, Little Eva and Simon Legree. Primordial images rather than living persons, they emerge mysteriously from the collective unconscious and pass, scarcely mediated by her almost transparent text, into the public domain, to which, like all authentic popular literature they properly belong.

Similarly, the scenes which stay with us forever seem as archetypal and oneiric as those protagonists: Eliza leaping from icefloe to icefloe in pursuit of freedom, or Eva, on the verge of maturity, dying a death lingering enough not just to convert her demure black anti-type, Topsy, and her Byronic father, but to extort tears from generations of readers. Eliza's scene is shorter than we can even believe—like a fragmentary dream dreamed in the moment before waking; while Eva's is described in considerable detail; but both have the realer-than-real vividness of hallucinations:

There was a sound in that chamber, first of one who stepped quickly. It was Miss Ophelia, who had resolved to sit up all night with her little charge, and who, at the turn of the night, had discerned what experienced nurses significantly call "a change." The outer door was quickly

23

opened, and Tom, who was watching outside, was on the alert, in a moment.

"Go for the doctor, Tom! lose not a moment," said Miss Ophelia; and, stepping across the room, she rapped at St. Clare's door.

"Cousin," she said, "I wish you would come."

Those words fell on his heart like clods upon a coffin. Why did they? He was up and in the room in an instant, and bending over Eva, who still slept.

What was it he saw that made his heart stand still? Why was no word spoken between the two? Thou canst say, who hast seen that same expression on the face dearest to thee;—that look indescribable, hopeless, unmistakable, that says to thee that thy beloved is no longer thine.

On the face of the child, however, there was no ghastly imprint,—only a high and almost sublime expression,—the over-shadowing presence of spiritual natures, the dawing of immortal life in that childish soul...

...The child lay panting on her pillows, as one exhausted,—the large clear eyes rolled up and fixed. Ah, what said those eyes, that spoke so much of heaven? Earth was past, and earthly pain; but so solemn, so mysterious, was the triumphant brightness of that face, that it checked even the sobs of sorrow. They pressed around her, in breathless stillness.

"Eva," said St. Clare, gently.

She did not hear.

"O, Eva, tell us what you see? What is it?" said her father.

A bright, a glorious smile passed over her face, and she said, brokenly,—"O! love,—joy,—peace!" gave one sigh, and passed from death unto life!

24

"Farewell, beloved child! the bright, eternal doors have closed after thee; we shall see thy sweet face no more. O, woe for them who watched thy entrance into heaven, when they shall wake and find only the cold gray sky of daily life, and thou gone forever."

What haunts us more, however, is the scene of Uncle Tom being beaten to death by Simon Legree and his Black henchmen, Sambo and Quimbo. But this is as it should be, since, Mrs. Stowe has told us, that scene came to her in Church, a wordless vision of horror which she could only exorcize by writing the entire book.

Legree drew in a long breath; and, suppressing his rage, took Tom by the arm, and, approaching his face almost to his, said, in a terrible voice, "Hark 'e, Tom!—ye think, 'cause I've let you off before, I don't mean what I say; but this time, I've *made up my mind* and counted the cost. You've always stood it out agin' me: now, I'll *conquer ye, or kill ye*!—one or t'other. I'll count every drop of blood there is in you, and take 'em, one by one, till ye give up!"

Finally, however, *all* of these key scenes seem visions without words, dreams or nightmares which have long possessed our sleep, though we did not know this until we encountered them waking on the pages of *Uncle Tom's Cabin*. It scarcely matters then that the passages in which they are evoked are among the worst written (by conventional literary standards) in the book: shrill to the point of hysteria, sickly sweet to the verge of nausea—yet magically moving, transcending somehow not just the ordinary criteria of taste, but of credibility itself.

The attempts of certain high-minded critics to save the book by rejecting these scenes or disavowing the mythic personae at their center (like Ellen Moers, for instance, who finds the minstrel show character Topsy a "brilliantly original creation" but rejects "treacly little Eva," and is uneasy with Tom) are completely beside the point. One suspects that such critics have never really read the book Mrs. Stowe really wrote, much less dissolved in tears when little Eva cries out in defense of slavery, "It makes for so many more around us to love"; or Uncle Tom breathes in the ear of the white boy, arrived too late to save him, "I loves every creatur', every whar!—it's nothing *but* love! O Mas'r George! what a thing 'tis to be a Christian!" The exclamation points and underlining are essential to the embarrassing text; and our own post-Christian dismay at finding ourselves vulnerable to so grossly sentimental an appeal serves only to increase the effect.

Even more difficult to accept these days are certain of Mrs. Stowe's assumptions about the nature and destiny of Black Americans, assumptions which radical Black leaders have taught us to regard as demeaning and unjust. Yet three of the enduring archetypal characters in her novel are Negroes, as seems only fair in light of the fact that, for better or worse, it was Mrs. Stowe who invented American Blacks for the imagination of the whole world. Before *Uncle Tom's Cabin*, they existed as historical, demographic, economic facts, their existence acknowledged but not felt with the passion and intensity we accord what moves through our dreams as well as our waking lives.

Afterwards, things were different; for Tom, Eliza and Topsy at least were immediately translated from the pages of Mrs. Stowe's book to the deep psyches of us all, Europeans and Americans, Whites and Blacks. Of the astonishing number of Afro-American characters she created, old and young, male and female, evil, good and merely indifferent, many remain mythologically inert; some indeed, being little more than variations on standard minstrel show types: comic darkies brought on for comic relief. But these three pressing relentlessly onward to their inevitable Endings—a bittersweet martyrdom which finds triumph in death, a final escape to freedom, and redemption to a life of Christian service—have survived the fiction in which they appear; becoming, for better or worse, models, archetypal grids through which we perceive the Negroes around us, and they perceive themselves. Among the "Good Niggers" of our literature, only Mark Twain's Jim has achieved a comparable mythological status, the Wilderness companion of the white runaway from civilization, originally conceived as a Red Man but converted in *Huckleberry Finn* into a Black.

2 Uncle Tom as White Mother

There has come into existence in the years since Mrs. Stowe first burst on an adoring world, a mythological "Bad Nigger" as compelling and memorable as Mrs. Stowe's "Good Nigger" or Mark Twain's Jim. This Shadow figure of the Black Rapist I cannot help suspecting already lurked in her own individual unconscious, as it lurked in the collective unconscious of the American people as a whole—erupting even before the Civil War in rumors of the violation of White Women by Black Males and consequent riots in the streets, like one that had occurred in Cincinnati while Mrs. Stowe was living there and learning the few facts she knew at first hand about White-Black relations in the South. But committed to making a case for abolition, she left the evocation of that Nightmare Archetype to later writers, both White and Black, to whom Jim seemed irrelevant and Uncle Tom an abominable lie: to Thomas Dixon, Jr., for instance, on the one side, and Richard Wright and Eldridge Cleaver on the other.

She was not, let it be understood, however genteel, squeamish about alluding to sexual relations between Blacks and Whites. Inter-ethnic rape is, in fact, a major theme in her sadomasochistic masterpiece—as central as inter-ethnic flagellation, which she eroticized to the point where it seems merely another version of sexual violation. But strategic considerations impelled her to deal exclusively with the rape or attempted rape of Black girls by White men, servants by masters. Toward the novel's conclusion, for instance, there is a long section which alternates descriptions of Tom's brutalization and death under the lash of Simon Legree with scenes in which the same Legree pursues through a decaying plantation house his former slave mistress, the aging and half-mad Emmeline, and Cassy, a beautiful and young quadroon, whom he hopes to make her successor.

Before that double climax, Cassy has managed to tell to Tom her earlier erotic misadventures with White lovers and masters—a melodramatic enough tale which begins like an idyllic romance and ends in betrayal, insanity and murder. It constitutes in fact a sketch for a whole other novel, which Mrs. Stowe never wrote, though it has been attempted scores of times since, the last time perhaps as recently as 1955 in Robert Penn Warren's *Band of Angels*. In any case, both Cassy's story and Emmeline's have disappeared from the memory of the common reader as totally as has the Quaker Household. In these instances, however, selective amnesia sets in not because they are too "allegorical," but because they are too "novelistic," i.e., dependent for their credibility on psychological "realism" rather than hallucinatory vividness.

It is, I suppose, for similar reasons that Little Eva's Bad Mother, Marie St. Clare, self-pitying, hypochondriacal, destructive to all around her, has also been forgotten by the popular audience. Her husband, Augustine, more "womanly" than she, which is to say, more sensitive and loving, but impotent and doomed, has fared a little better. He is remembered, however, not at the center of the "novelistic" scenes which he shares with his wife, but on the periphery of more mythic ones dominated by his dying daughter, in her relationship with those other archetypal *personae*, Topsy and Tom.

Inevitable as it is, I must confess I regret the disappearance of Mrs. St. Clare from collective memory; for in some sense she is worthy to stand with such other avatars of the neurotic Southern Lady as Faulkner's Mrs. Compson or even Margaret Mitchell's Scarlett O'Hara. Returning to the book, I sometimes find myself in fact flipping to the pages in which Mrs. Stowe, after having pinned her down in a twice-repeated phrase ("...she consisted of a fine figure, a pair of splendid eyes and a hundred thousand dollars..."), proceeds to show Marie St. Clare's failure as a wife, a mother and a mistress of Black servants, her total lack of sympathy for others compounded by monumental self-pity. Of all the voices in the book, it is her self-justifying whine that I find it hardest to exorcize, shuddering at the cruelty it barely conceals as I never shudder at the naked histrionics of Legree: "So you just see...what you've got to manage. A household without any rule; where servants have it all their own way, do what they please, and have what they please, except so far as I, with my feeble health, have kept up governments. I keep my cowhide about, and sometimes I do lay it on; but the exertion is always too much for me..."

Yet I know that however successful "novelistically," this portrait of the absolute Bad Mother fails to become mythic like that of the Wicked Slavedriver. It arises not out of the part of Mrs. Stowe's undermind continuous with the collective unconscious, but out of repressed resentments, very private and personal, a clash of domestic life styles. The vicious precision of the portrayal betrays its motivation: the need of a brilliant, homely, harried Northern housewife to take revenge on her spoiled, indolent and, alas, beautiful sisters of the South. Nonetheless, in this book addressed primarily to the Good Mothers of America, there is no sketch of a Good Mother of comparable intensity and scale.

Rachel Halliday stands outside the main action, like those other kindly maternal souls Eliza encounters on her flight; and Eliza herself dominates only what becomes as the book progresses a sub-plot, a digression from the main story of martyrdom and redemption. Even in her single archetypal scene, she functions primarily not as a Mother but as the Maiden in Flight. Had she been captured by the slave trader, Haley (it is clear), that would have meant not merely her separation from her little son, so sketchily rendered that it seems hard to believe the bundle of rags she clutches to her beautiful bosom contains a living child, but her own sexual degradation. She seems, in that scene, even less wife than mother, though Mrs. Stowe had earlier insisted on the pathos of her parting from her husband, George Harris, who is absent as she crosses the ice, i.e., absent from the mythic center of her plight; and he has therefore faded from collective memory as completely as his son.

More central, though finally not of true mythic resonance, are certain Good White Mothers dead before the main action of the novel begins. Returning as ghosts or divine messengers, they save their erring sons, if they repent in time (as in the case of Augustine St. Clare); or failing that, damn them for all eternity (as in the case of Simon Legree). There is something about the mysterious connection of damnation and motherly love which troubles, as well as titillates Mrs. Stowe; who attempts, therefore, to explain it in theological terms, equating mothers with the God of the Old Testament. "Ye who have wondered to hear, in the same evangel, that 'God is love,' and that 'God is a consuming fire,' see you now how to the soul resolved in evil, perfect love is the most dreadful torture . . ."

There is, however, one spokesman in her book, who would save even Simon Legree, and seems therefore to represent all in the author which yearns toward "womanly" forgiveness and love as endless accommodation. "He ain't done me no real harm," the dying Tom says of the man who has struck him down, foaming in dark passion, "only opened the gates of the kingdom for me; that's all'', thus proving himself once more as he had already proved himself at the bedside of martyred Little Eva, the book's ultimate Good Mother; which is to say, a secret self-portrait of the author. That Uncle Tom is really a white mother in blackface and drag others have at least dimly perceived before, Helen Papashvily and William R. Taylor most recently; though Charlotte Bronte seems to have guessed the ill-kept secret first, observing that "Mrs. Stowe had felt the iron of slavery enter into her heart from childhood upwards."

The implication is clear. Merely by having been born a woman in her time and place, more specifically, a white daughter of New England Puritans, Mrs. Stowe had been born in her deepest self-consciousness a slave—forbidden by a law more absolute than the statutes of legislatures any recourse from patriarchal power except submission and prayer. And it is certainly true that what released in her the vision of suffering and forgiveness unto death out of which her book was born was her awareness of that plight. Though *Uncle Tom's Cabin* has been praised for its "realism," its fidelity to history, and though Mrs. Stowe herself came to think of it as more document than fiction, what moves and convinces us in its pages is not scholarly fact but fantasy born of paranoia, itself bred by oppression.

No one, except in dreams, has ever been as good as Tom, as pure as Eva, as demonic as Topsy, as unremittingly evil as Simon Legree. But insofar as we all feel ourselves obsessed or oppressed, we all dream such dreams; and Mrs. Stowe, like other enduring popular authors, permits us the luxury of re-dreaming them *awake*. She was gifted with easy access not just to her own unconscious but to that of the mass audience, whose archetypal figments she believed in with a poetic faith bordering on madness. She was, moreover, blessedly ignorant of the facts of life among Negro slaves, except as she could reconstruct it by analogy with the plight of her sex. Apparently, however, that analogy did not occur to her until illness, which is to say, "an act of God," had carried off one of her own children. "It was at his dying bed..." she wrote in a letter describing the loss of her son, "that I learned how a poor slave may feel."

Though an advocate of women's rights, she was not a hardcore feminist like her mad sister, who believed that Christ was about to return, ushering in a matriarchal age in which she would function as his Vice-Regent. Mrs. Stowe's initial quarrel was less with men than with their patricarchal God, who, like the most arrogant of slavemasters, tore children from the arms of their mothers; so that her book is as much about death as it is about slavery. Yet as she wrote, she became more and more possessed by the equation of White Women and Black Slaves as victims of White Men and the God they had created in their own image. No wonder, then, that in her book, not just Uncle Tom, but all good Negroes seem more female than male, at least as she and her age interpreted those terms.

The Anglo-Saxon she associates with the mythological characteristics of men, "stern, inflexible, energetic... dominant, commanding," contrasting them with "the African, naturally patient, timid and unenterprising... not naturally daring and enterprising, but home-loving and affectionate." And of Uncle Tom, in particular, she remarks at one point, that he possessed "to the full, the gentle, domestic heart, which, woe for them! has been a peculiar characteristic of his unhappy race." It is this shamanistic shifting of sex roles which so annoys James Baldwin, a rather improbable spokesman for Black *machismo*, who thinks of it as a kind of symbolic castration. But only so could Mrs. Stowe neutralize Tom enough to make possible the evocation of him, old (but we are never sure *how* old he really is), black and motherly, holding the frail body of a dying White girl in his arms.

Iconographically, certain of his scenes with Little Eva are not very different from later ones portraying the Black Rapist carrying his unconscious pale victim toward defloration and death. Only the tone is altered and the symbolic role of the Negro; so that the resonances it stirs are not those associated with the primordial images of Kore, the Eternal Daughter, ravished by her Dark Father, the King of Hell. It seems rather one more version of what has been called the "Protestant Pieta," reminding us of Cordelia dead in the arms of Lear, or Little Nell in those of her grandfather. Neither Shakespeare, however, or Dickens (as Dostoevski perceived and made manifest in *The Possessed*)

35

quite managed to avoid overtones of incestuous passion debouching in murder. But these seem quite absent from Mrs. Stowe's recension of the myth, in which Tom represents not the impotent and resentful father but the Blessed Male Mother of a virgin Female Christ.

All feelings associated with rape have been transferred to the final archetypal scene in which Tom has become the passive victim, and his ravisher, in a strategic mythological inversion, the book's most *macho*, Anglo-Saxon and lustful character, Legree, who is assisted, to be sure, by Sambo and Quimbo, representing everything in White nightmares of Black sexuality and aggression which Uncle Tom denies: "The two gigantic negroes that now laid hold of Tom...might have formed no unapt personification of the powers of darkness." The vision with which it all began and which came to Mrs. Stowe just after Communion, becomes here truly obscene, as Legree "foaming with rage" and determined to assert his ultimate power as absolute master ("And isn't he MINE? Can't I do what I like with him?" he cries over Tom's fallen body), consummates what it is tempting to think of as connubial murder and rape. Meanwhile, Tom, like some dutiful middle class White Christian wife of the time, can only answer male brutality with submissive prayer: "Mas'r, if you was sick, or in trouble, or dying, I'd *give* ye my heart's blood..."

Being a good Christian lady, Mrs. Stowe refuses to describe treatment of that scene in detail, leaving it to our pornographic imaginations: "What man has nerve to do," she explains piously, "man has not nerve to hear..." But, of course, it is all the more effective for that very reason: not just satisfying the mass audience's need for righteous indignation and sadomasochistic titillation; but establishing that identification of "nigger" with woman, woman with "nigger," which made the progress from abolitionism to feminism inevitable for certain of Mrs. Stowe's readers, whatever her conscious intent.

It is harder to believe that Mrs. Stowe's great potboiler was responsible for the outbreak of the Civil War, though Abraham Lincoln thought so, or at least was moved to say so in her presence. For a while, readers on both sides of the Mason Dixon line seem to have read it with equal pleasure; and it began to divide North from South (after all, Mrs. Stowe had deliberately made her most arrant villain a New Englander by birth) only when it was taken up by apologists for and against slavery. To be sure, there are political implications everywhere in Mrs. Stowe's dream-book; but like all dreams it told its dreamers only what they already knew, leading, therefore, not to a change of heart and mind but greater self-awareness. The outcome of such dreams in the waking world is therefore not action but literature; precisely such a work in fact as *Uncle Tom's Cabin*, which may have helped Americans, Northern and Southern, *perceive* differently the war they were bound in any case to fight, but cannot have hastened its coming.

On its conscious level, Mrs. Stowe's novel neither preached nor foresaw a War between the States. What she hoped for was the voluntary freeing of slaves by individual owners, the spread of education among those thus freed; and their consequent emigration to Africa, where they would take over the Christianizing of that continent which White missionaries had begun. What she feared was a general slave uprising, like that in Haiti and San Domingo. After all, Mrs. Stowe was not only a chiliastic Christian, but the child of a Revolutionary Age, in which the oppressed everywhere were turning against their masters. That movement, which peaked in 1848, inspired almost simultaneously two literary responses, one profoundly European, the other peculiarly American: Marx and Engels' *Communist Manifesto* and her *Uncle Tom's Cabin*. If, according to the first, the spectre haunting Europe was Communism, according to the second, the spectre haunting America was Black Revolt. None of the characters in *Uncle Tom's Cabin*, however, really embody this threat, certainly not Tom. Even George Harris, her single Negro militant, is not permitted to fire the gun he raises against his White pursuers; and when the diabolical Sambo and Quimbo turn against their brutal master, it is to espouse Christianity rather than bloodshed, arson, murder and rape. In her second novel, *Dred: A Tale of the Great Dismal Swamp*, Mrs. Stowe attempted to tell a story of Slave Rebellion, but the result was a failure—mythologically inert, structurally confused, moving to no one.

In fact, Mrs. Stowe never again created a fiction which touched the popular imagination. Scholars and critics, uneasy with *Uncle Tom's Cabin*, like to pretend that toward the end of her writing career she succeeded in producing better books, *Oldtown Folks*, for instance. But it is hard to believe that any ordinary reader has ever loved such bloodless evocations of New England life, much less shuddered or wept over them, shamelessly out of control. Only once (by God's grace, she would have said) was she permitted to peer into the darkness of the American undermind and to redeem for daylight the phantasms, Black and White, who inhabit it, phantasms to whom she gave the local habitation and the names by which we have identified them ever since.

For the rest of her life, she lived the life of a celebrity, a little pompous and something of a fool, as in her self-styled defense of Lady Byron; really an attack on the incestuous Lord Byron whom she extravagantly admired and passionately despised. In the end, she went quite dotty—seeing her drowned favorite son on the streets of Hartford long after he was dead; sneaking up behind her respectable neighbors to shout "Boo!", or invading their houses while they slept to sing hymns at the top of her voice.

All the while, however, her reputation kept increasing, her single great work amended, continued, in some sense, *completed* by anonymous or forgotten hacks. Even before her death, the deathless characters she had first imagined, Tom, Eliza, Topsy, Eva, had ceased to belong to her, entering the world not of high literature but of popular entertainment, in which all goods are held in common. During her last years, her name may have been known to everyone, but fewer and fewer knew it from having read her book rather than having seen the "Tom plays," which proliferated throughout the world. Moved by curiosity, she herself once attended a performance, peering through the closed curtains of a private box, though she had condemned theatre and opera, along with swearing, gambling, smoking, slavery and hard drink, in the pages of *Uncle Tom's Cabin* itself.

Even Henry James, remembering her tale in *A Small Boy and Others*, which he published in 1913, recalls it more vividly as theatre than as printed text, evoking side by side with the name of Mrs. Stowe those of actresses who had played Eliza, Cassy, Topsy and Eva, as well as that of P.T. Barnum, at whose American Museum he had first watched it side by side with midgets, giants, a

counterfeit mermaid and a Black ex-slave who claimed
to be the world's oldest woman. He ends his account by
assuring us that he enjoyed the play only as "camp":
"However, the point exactly was that we attended this
spectacle just in order *not* to be beguiled, just in order
to enjoy with ironic detachment and, at the very most,
to be amused ourselves at our sensibility should it prove
to have been trapped and caught."

It is clear nonetheless that despite his retrospective
irony his sensibility had been "trapped and caught";
and in speculating on the story's insidious appeal, he
notes—for perhaps the first time in critical discourse—a
quality which distinguishes all popular art from high
art, namely, its ability to move from one medium to
another without loss of intensity or alteration of meaning: its independence, in short, of the form in which it
is first rendered. "Letters," James wrote, "here, lan-
guished unconscious, and Uncle Tom, instead of making even one of the cheap short cuts through the
medium in which books breathe, even as fishes in water,
went gaily roundabout it altogether, as if a fish, a wonderful 'leaping' fish, had simply flown through the air.
This feat accomplished, the surprising creature could
naturally fly anywhere, and one of the first things it did
was thus to flutter down on every stage, literally without
exception, in America and Europe."

Like many popular genres, however, the popular
theatre of the nineteenth century in which Mrs. Stowe's
"wonderful 'leaping' fish" had fluttered down, proved
a transitory rather than a final form—giving way to
movies, radio and T.V., which more quickly reached an
even larger audience. I was born just too late ever to
have seen a "Tom Play" on stage; and I know them,
therefore, as they are preserved in films: performed, for

instance, before Yul Brynner as King of Siam in *The King and I*; or glimpsed over the shoulder of Shirley Temple, in a moving picture whose name I have forgotten, though not the scene in which the ingenue as Little Eva, wins over her beloved's mother, hitherto as hostile to theatre and actresses as Mrs. Stowe herself.

I am more directly familiar with the fictional spin-offs from *Uncle Tom's Cabin*, which began to appear side by side with the dramatic versions, responses in novel form by various hands. Such unauthorized sequels to her best-seller may have seemed to Mrs. Stowe an infringement of copyright and a threat to her livelihood. But like Cervantes and Dickens before her, she had to endure them as a consequence of her kind of success, learning the hard way that in the realm of popular art, books are as independent of their authors as of their medium.

In any case, anti-Tom books like *Aunt Phillis's Cabin; or Southern Life As It Is, Uncle Tom's Cabin As It Is, Uncle Tom In England; or, Proof That White's Black,* never attracted a large audience—not so much because their authors were untalented (a couple were, in fact, already immensely popular), as because they failed to understand that the book they sought to "answer" was a dream-fantasy even more concerned with death, sexual purity and the bourgeois home than the Fugitive Slave Law.

3 The Anti-Tom Novel and the First Great War: Thomas Dixon Jr. and D.W. Griffith

Only when a writer appeared as obsessed and visionary as Mrs. Stowe could her compelling images of race and sex be replaced by others of quite different significance. That writer was Thomas Dixon, Jr., whose name is little known at the moment, though his novels sold millions of copies in the early twentieth century, precisely because they seemed the long-awaited response to Mrs. Stowe. "It is an epoch-making book," one critic wrote of *The Leopard's Spots*, "and a worthy successor to *Uncle Tom's Cabin*. It is superior in power of thought and graphic description..." Others, however, appalled at Dixon's vilification of Black Men and his defense of the Ku Klux Klan, attacked him with a fury equal to that earlier turned against Mrs. Stowe, from the other side. Accusing him of being "the high priest of lawlessness, the prophet of anarchy," and a stirrer-up of "enmity between race and race," they called in righteous indignation for the censorship of his books.

To Dixon, however, such latter-day detractors seemed of little importance, since he had taken on the dead and sanctified patron saint of them all. Mrs. Stowe had had the first word in the Great Debate, a word that had captured the heart of the world; but he was determined to have the last, and to couch it in the fictional form, melodramatic and sentimental, which he had learned from her. It seems doubtful, indeed, if he would ever have become a novelist at all without her example and provocation. Though not yet forty when he began to write *The Leopard's Spots*, he had already been a farmer, a scholarship student at Johns Hopkins University, a drop-out vainly trying to make it on the New York stage, a lawyer, a legislator, a Minister of the Gospel, a pamphleteer attacking strong drink and "infidels" like Robert Ingersoll, finally, a popular lecturer.

It was in fact "During one of his lecturing tours," as his biographer, Raymond A. Cook, tells us, that "Dixon attended a dramatization of Harriet Beecher Stowe's *Uncle Tom's Cabin*. Angered by what seemed to him a great injustice to the South, he could hardly keep from leaping to his feet and denouncing the drama as false. Finally, when the performance was over, he rose with tears in his eyes and vowed bitterly that he would someday tell the 'true story' of the South." That "true story" became a trilogy of novels, *The Leopard's Spots* (1902), *The Clansman* (1905) and *The Traitor* (1907); after which, though the threat of "racial mongrelization" continued to obsess him, Dixon directed his fictional fire chiefly against his other favorite bugaboos: socialism, pacifism, feminism, monarchism and booze.

Never, in any case, did he write except on behalf of what seemed to him a worthy cause. "I have made no effort to write literature," he declared. "I had no ambition to shine as a literary gymnast... My sole purpose in writing was to reach and influence the minds of millions. I had a message and I wrote it as vividly and simply as I knew how." It is an anti-aesthetic credo not

44

unlike that of Mrs. Stowe, who once said of *Uncle Tom's Cabin* that she "no more thought of style or literary excellence than the mother who rushes into the street and cries for help to save her children from a burning house, thinks of the teachings of the rhetorician or the elocutionist." To be sure, his controlling metaphor is more pastoral than matriarchal; but like Mrs. Stowe, he understood that to win the Great Audience one had to project their irrational wishes and fears in "pictures" or "visions," detachable from the words in which they were transmitted.

What made his task easier was the fact that, like her, he prized female virginity and the integrity of the home, embodying the one in the image of the Spotless Maiden and the other in that of the Holy Mother. "Every woman," he has one of his more sympathetic characters declare, "is something divine to me. I think of God as a woman, not a man—a great loving Mother of all life..." For him, however, the supreme threat to these avatars of the Feminine is not, as Mrs. Stowe, the slavetrader and slavedriver, but the half-bestial Black Man released from all patriarchal restraints.

Dixon is finally no defender of slavery, granting that Emancipation was necessary for the development of a united Nation. But it was unforgiveable for the North, he argues, in the name of "Reconstruction," to make Black ex-slaves into the Masters of their former owners—rather than persuading them to leave en masse for Africa, or to live in segregated communities as eternal inferiors. He is fond of quoting Lincoln as having said, "I believe there is a physical difference between the white and black races which will forever forbid their living together on terms of political and social equality..." He admired Lincoln, in fact, without reservation;

claiming that he was really a "Southerner," by which he meant just such a descendant of Scotch-Irish peasants as himself and the organizers of the Klan.

Dixon liked to refer to those original Klansmen, the heroes of his books, as "Anglo-Saxons," though the Anglo Saxon Aristocracy of the Old South would have spurned such ethnic confusion. Even as Mrs. Stowe pleaded the cause of women in the guise of attacking slavery, Dixon pleaded the cause of the Scotch-Irish in the name of White Supremacy. And like Mrs. Stowe, he managed to translate his peculiar plight into universal images; so that his "redneck" fantasies of nigger-hating and lynch law appealed not only to his "redneck" brethren, but to declassed WASP plantation owners fighting to establish a New South, and even to recent immigrants from Eastern or Southern Europe confronting free Negroes in the cities of the Midwest and Northeast.

He did not, however, really know what he was doing at first, beyond burlesquing Mrs. Stowe's masterpiece. The working title of *The Leopard's Spots* was *The Rise of Simon Legree*; and though the name of the book was changed, Legree remains of considerable importance. We learn, for instance, how he survived the Civil War: "he shaved clean, and...wore dresses for two years, did housework...''; and how, afterwards, he prepared for his new career as a capitalist and sexual exploiter of factory girls: "He wore a silk hat and a new suit of clothes made by a fashionable tailor...His teeth that once were pointed like the fangs of a wolf had been filed by a dentist...''

Other characters out of *Uncle Tom's Cabin* are similarly travestied, especially the now grown-up son of

Eliza, renamed "George" by Dixon, though Mrs. Stowe has called him "Harry." Handsome and almost white, George Harris enters the scene as a Harvard graduate, scholar, poet and protege of the champion of Black Liberation, the Honorable Everett Lowell, with whose daughter he falls in love. When he asks for her hand, however, his liberal New England sponsor turns cold and hostile, initiating a dialogue in which the deep fears that Dixon and the mass audience of the early twentieth century had left unspoken, find their classic expression:

> Harris winced and sprang to his feet, trembling with passion. "I see," he sneered; "the soul of Simon Legree has at last become the soul of the nation. The South expresses the same luminous truth with a little more clumsy brutality. But their way is after all more merciful. The human body becomes unconscious at the touch of an oil-fed flame in sixty seconds. Your methods are more refined and more hellish in cruelty. You have trained my ears to hear, eyes to see, hands to touch and heart to feel, that you might torture with the denial of every cry of body and soul and roast me in the flames of impossible desires for time and eternity!"
>
> "That will do now. There's the door!" thundered Lowell, with a gesture of stern emphasis. "I happen to know the important fact that a man or woman of Negro ancestry, though a century removed, will suddenly breed back to a pure Negro child, thick-lipped, kinky-headed, flat-nosed, black-skinned. One drop of your blood in my family could push it backward three thousand years in history. If you were able to win her consent, a thing un-thinkable, I would do what old Virginius did in the Roman Forum—kill her with my own hand, rather than see her sink in your arms into the black waters of a Negroid life! Now go!"

It is not, of course, with "fact" that we are dealing

here (though many reputable anthropologists of the day would have insisted that Everett Lowell spoke "scientific truth") but fantasy: a fantasy based on fear of "racial mongrelization" resulting from Emancipation, which presumably freed Black males not just from slavery but from the restraints hereto imposed on their lust for White women. Though Mrs. Stowe refuses to confess the existence of that lust (much less of a corresponding yearning on the part of White women for Black males), the popular mind had long been haunted by a suspicion of both. Yet not until fifty years after the Civil War, did a new Myth of Miscegenation replace the older one of Black females sexually exploited by their White masters, who then turned over the mulatto offspring they had thus engendered to be whipped or sold away from their mothers.

In *Uncle Tom's Cabin*, there is, to be sure, an equivocal icon, transmitted by the Tom Plays to every stage of the world, portraying frail White female flesh enfolded in the brawny arms of a Black male. But since the flesh belongs to the eternally virginal Little Eva and the arms to a castrated "motherly" Tom, it all seems safe enough. "It was Tom's greatest delight," Mrs. Stowe tells us, "to carry her frail form in his arms... now up and down her room, now out into the veranda..." And when her weaker White father protests that this is his obligation and privilege, Eva answers, "Oh, Papa, let Tom take me... He carries me so strong."

If there are erotic overtones in that final phrase: *"He carries me so strong,"* Mrs. Stowe seems to have been unaware of them; though, indeed, she registers through Miss Ophelia, an old maid New England cousin of Augustine St. Clare, the Northerner's horror of any physical contact between the races. And that explicit horror joined to the implicit eros of the encounter, Dixon, moved by God knows what sexual envy and fear, raises to its final intensity in *The Leopard's Spots* and *The Clansman*, converting Mrs. Stowe's innocent idyll into a tableau of murderous lust.

Ever since Samuel Richardson's *Clarissa*, rape had been a staple of best-selling female fiction. But Victorian gentility had removed it from center-stage, compelling writers to hint at it as threat or fact, rather than describe it candidly. Mrs. Stowe, for instance, does not let Simon Legree consummate the White-Black violation of Emmeline, though she is willing to portray his pursuit of her. And even Dixon is a little squeamish about portraying Black-White rape in detail; so that in his first novel, he keeps the archetypal scene off-stage. We hear the nigger-hating father of Little Flora, the fated White victim, warn her, "But, baby, don't you dare go nigh er nigger...no more'n you would a rattlesnake." Then the author intervenes to inform us, "She believed with her child's simple faith that all nature was as innocent as her own heart..."; at which point, she disappears to return as a corpse: "her clothes torn to shreds and stained with blood." "It was too plain, the terrible crime that had been committed," Dixon adds, lest we have missed the point; but, of course, we have not.

Later in *The Clansman* Dixon is more explicit, though this time he renders the scene only at second hand, as its Black villain Gus confesses under hypnotism, to a crime whose "sullied" victim, has by that time committed suicide, jumping from a cliff hand-in-hand with her approving mother. "His thick lips were drawn upward in an ugly leer and his sinister bead-eye gleamed like a gorilla's. A single fierce leap and the black claws clutched the air slowly as if sinking into the soft white throat." Gus's execution by the listening jury of Clansmen follows immediately, but is not described; as if one image of ultimate violence were enough to satisfy the self-righteous sadism of the audience: rape *or* lynching, but not both.

In *The Leopard's Spots*, in which the rape was kept out of sight, the lynching had been recounted at some length: "They reached the spot where the child's body had been found. They tied the screaming, praying Negro to a live pine and piled around his body a great heap of dead wood and saturated it with oil. And then they poured oil on his clothes..." Such "insane brutality" is, apparently, too much even for Dixon (who had witnessed such a scene as a child), though he cannot forebear recounting it, entrusting his reservations to a Klan leader impotent to stop the mob he has earlier incited. Such scenes are in any event essential to his story: the equivalent of the flogging-to-death of Tom, from which Mrs. Stowe's book began. In Dixon, however, the balance of ambivalence in the face of such horror has shifted—so that self-satisfaction outweighs indignation and pity.

Nonetheless, those icons of primordial terror, have in his work, outlived what is merely documentary or fictional or personal. The mass audience soon forgot Dixon's travesties of characters out of *Uncle Tom's Cabin*, his evocation of historical figures like Lincoln and Thaddeus Stevens, his editorial asides about state's rights, as well as the single love story he told over and over, in which some clean-cut, clean-limbed Son of the Old South delivers from her father's tyranny his incredibly beautiful Beloved, even as he rises to leadership in the ranks of the Klan. But his mythology of rape and lynching on the margin where two alien cultures meet evokes images which haunt us still in a world vexed by even more exacerbated confrontations of White and Black, White and Brown, White and Yellow, White and Red, Yellow and Black, Black and Red, Brown and Yellow.

Like Mrs. Stowe's, moreover, his novels became from the start occasions for other books, written in rebuttal, and translations into other media, from which he, unlike her (who earned not a penny from the Tom Plays), profited immensely. Similarly, in the field of fiction, his anti-Tom Trilogy has been replaced in popular esteem by Margaret Mitchell's *Gone With the Wind*, which it helped inspire. And that novel in turn has been made into a film, that film re-presented as a T.V. event viewed by a larger audience than has ever watched anything in the medium except for Alex Haley's anti-anti-Tom epic, *Roots*.

Earlier anti-anti-Tom books, however, written like *Roots* by Negroes, have fared less well. The very names of novels like Sutton E. Griggs' *The Hindered Hand*, which appeared in 1905, and J.W. Grant's *Out of the Darkness; or Diabolism and Destiny*, published in 1909, are known now only to specialists in early Black American Literature. Parochial attempts to present the case for racial intermarriage or social equality and to set straight the record on Reconstruction, they failed not only because they lack literary skill and mythic resonance; but because the backlash of white guilt and self-hatred on which Haley would capitalize, lay still far in the future.

What moved the popular audience in the ten years between the publication of *The Clansman* and the beginning of World War I, were dramatic versions of Dixon's own book: first of all, the play which he himself made of *The Clansman* and which he marketed by soliciting pre-production plaudits from the then Secretary of State, John Hay, and Albert Bigelow Paine, the future biographer of Mark Twain. When it finally was produced, however, even in the South, more soberminded critics condemned it as "a riot breeder... designed to excite rage and race hatred"; and in some Northern cities, there were indeed riots. But on the whole, the box-office response was tumultuously favorable, leading Dixon to speculate that it might ultimately be seen by ten million spectators. Sitting in the theatre, moreover, he was thrilled as no novelist in his lonely study ever can be. "There," he wrote later, "I saw, felt and heard, and touched the hands of my readers and their united heart beat lifted me to the heights."

In some ways, however, the stage was too limited for the epic effects he dreamed. How could four horsemen galloping across a flimsy set represent the glory and terror of the assembled Klan riding to the rescue of White Womanhood? Besides, there was a new medium through which he could reach an even larger audience, achieve even greater fame and fortune. He set to work almost immediately, therefore, on a movie scenario; but when, in 1911, he began his search for a producer, he found at first only timid enterpreneurs scared to attempt so ambitious and controversial a project. Fortunately, however, his script fell into the hands of D.W. Griffith, a young director with ambitions as boundless as his own and ready, at precisely that point, to try his hand at a major work. Besides, Griffith, the son of a Confederate officer, and an unreconstructed Southerner, was possessed by the same myth of the

South that cued Dixon's deepest fantasy. Moreover, he was equally responsive to popular taste. "...the peanuts-and-popcorn audience controlled Griffith," writes Karl Brown, a cameraman, who watched the shooting of the film, "and as long as he lived, thought and had his being with the strictest compliance with their unspoken wishes, he could do no wrong."

Brown had already read and hated Dixon's novel. "It wasn't much of a story," he comments, "Terribly biased, utterly unfair, the usual diatribe of a fire-eating Southerner, reverend or no reverend." And, as he guessed, Griffith exaggerated in the filming everything which had offended Brown to begin with; making the Black villains more villainous, the White heroes more unbelievably noble, the even Whiter heroines more passive, fluttering and ethereal. "There was nothing high-flown or arty about *The Clansman* as Griffith shot it," Brown concluded. "Everything was of the earth, earthy." But of course it *worked*, whipping its first audiences to frenzy, and making millionaires of both Griffith and Dixon.

Ironically, however, Dixon was to disappear in the shadow of Griffith, who thenceforward came to be thought of as America's greatest movie maker. The classic tribute to him and his film, ultimately called *The Birth of a Nation*, was written by James Agee in 1948, when the film was seldom shown for fear of boycotts and picket lines, and it took, therefore, considerable *chutzpah* to present. Agee is aware not only of the magnificence of the film, but of its status as anti-High Art, referring to Griffith as a "primitive: capable as only great and primitive artists can be, of...perceiving and perfecting the tremendous magical images that underlie the memory and imagination of entire peoples."

53

When Agee comes to specifying Griffith's tremendous "magical images," however, two of them turn out to have been borrowed from Dixon: "the ride of the Clansmen; the rapist and his victim among the dark leaves." Yet he seems unaware of Dixon's existence and fails, therefore, to understand why Griffith never again was able to project archetypes that have refused to fade from the mind of the world. It is not surprising that other critics, unsympathetic from the start, have persisted in ignoring that novelist. Yet on the morning after the opening of *The Birth of a Nation*, it was Dixon's intermission speech rather than Griffith's which the newspapers reported at length; since the aging novelist was better known than the young director, and the story still associated chiefly with him.

Dixon had in fact helped produce an earlier version, shot though never cut; and this time, too, he was involved from the start: holing up in New York with Griffith for many weeks of consultation, then shipping him off to Hollywood loaded down with his original screenplay plus the historical documents he had used in researching it. It was Dixon, too, who persuaded Griffith to change the name of the film to *The Birth of a Nation*, shouting across the cheers of the first night audience that *The Clansman* was "too tame a title for so powerful a story." Griffith has, moreover, left an account of the "vision" which came to him as he first read the novel: at the center of which shone the "flashing sword" of his father, old "Thunder Jake" Griffith, with which as a boy he had watched him threaten, half in jest, a cowering Negro; and he tells us further that he read it aloud to his company before shooting began. Certainly, anyone familiar with Dixon's novels, can recognize in the finished film specific borrowings from

The Leopard's Spots as well as *The Clansman*, however altered on the set (Griffith worked from no fixed script) or in the cutting room.

What chiefly survive in the new medium are Dixon's mythic versions of North and South, Male and Female, Black and White; and especially his vision of Reconstruction as an orgy of looting and rape, loosed in a world of gallantry and grace by greedy invaders and bewildered ex-slaves: a saturnalia subdued only by the Christian Knights of the Klan, whose fiery crosses betoken the end of Nightmare and the dawn of a new day. No one who has seen the Ride of the Klan in *The Birth of a Nation* can ever forget it: those silent hooves pounding as if forever through a dream landscape; the camera returning again and again to the hushed riders bent over the sweating backs of their horses, then cutting to their wives, mothers and daughters trapped in a house around which a horde of black devils swirls, banging against wall and door with rapacious hands. There is no doubt in the minds of any viewer about why the few old men trapped with them hold cocked pistols to the heads of their women. We have already seen the fate of white innocence, called this time "Little Sister," and this time driven over the edge of a cliff by the Black Rapist, Gus. Lifted from Dixon's novel, Gus becomes a more ultimate horror when played by a white man in blackface, dosed with hydrogen of peroxide until he foams at the mouth, like Legree at the point of smiting Uncle Tom.

Karl Brown has described the reaction of the first-night audience to that charge of the Klan: "the cheers began to arise from all over the packed house". And though more highminded film critics have ever since tended to deplore it, ("...here was the pattern for the

55

cheapest and most hollow film sensations," Jay Leyda writes, "the ornament of every film that hoped to stamp out all intellectual stimulus with a brutal physical impact..."), it has provided the model for a million B-movie rides to the rescue, in which, no matter how stereotyped, it never quite loses its primordial power. But no one has ever done it better than Griffith in *The Birth of a Nation*, at the climax of which audiences still go out of control.

I myself once saw, for example, the members of a Left Wing Cine Club in Athens, believers all in the equality of the races and the unmitigated evil of the Klan, rise to their feet at ten o'clock in the morning (the year was 1960, two wars and innumerable revolutions after the making of the film) to scream with bloodlust and approval equal to that of the racist first-nighters of 1915, as White Womanhood was once more delivered from the threat of Black Rape. It was not merely the magic of Griffith, that old "master of motion," which plunged them open-eyed first into then out of a Nightmare, in which God knows what ultimate enemies of their own were threatening what prized and virginal darlings, but the myths which he had inherited from Dixon, and which Dixon had somehow derived from Harriet Beecher Stowe, whose work, it should be added, the entire crew of the film knew even better than they did Dixon's. In fact, Karl Brown tells us, the exterior set of the small southern town, in which the action of *The Birth of a Nation* begins, was modelled on shared memories of the Tom Plays, a mythological setting in which Dixon's characters proved no less at home than Mrs. Stowe's.

There is something profoundly disturbing about the power of vulgar works like Dixon's and Griffith's to move us at a level beneath that of our conscious allegiances, religious or political. I can understand, therefore, why groups used in such works to symbolize Evil should protest their showing; and why organizations espousing doctrines which those works subvert should join in trying to ban them. Despite my distrust of all who believe themselves absolutely right and my unqualified opposition to censorship in any form, I can sympathize with the attempt of the NAACP to suppress *The Birth of a Nation*, for its "loathsome misrepresentations of colored people and the glorification of the hideous and murderous band of the Ku Klux Klan." But as a writer often considered controversial in my own time, I identify more with Griffith's rage at what he calls the "drooling travesty of sense" perpetrated "by ill minded censors and politicians...playing for the Negro vote."

In any case, such attempts at suppression did not, could not, cannot work. There is no way to censor troubled dreams, in which our otherwise unconfessed ambivalence about, say, the Emancipation of Black Slaves, finds symbolic expression; since such dreams are in the unconscious of all Americans, including white politicians and the Black voters for whom they claim to speak. It seems to me instructive that the NAACP which harried Dixon and Griffith in 1915, three decades later bestowed a special award on Butterfly MacQueen for acting out in the film version of *Gone With the Wind* a condescending stereotype of the "Good Nigger" quite compatible with the mythology of *The Clansman* and *The Birth of a Nation*.

4 The Anti-Tom Novel and the Great Depression: Margaret Mitchell's *Gone With the Wind*

Dixon, who lived to 1946, recognized his literary kinship to Margaret Mitchell, sending her a letter immediately after the publication of her novel to tell her how much it had moved him, and assuring her that he intended to write a booklength study of her work. In quick response, she acknowledged her indebtedness to *him*, explaining, "I was practically raised on your books and love them very much... When I was eleven years old I decided I would dramatize your book 'The Traitor'—and dramatize it I did in six acts ..." Unfortunately, Dixon suffered a cerebral hemmorhage shortly thereafter and so never managed to keep his promise. But one can easily imagine how sympathetically he would have responded to her view of Reconstruction as a total disaster and of the Klan as its necessary aftermath; as well as her portrayal of unspoiled Black American slaves as stupid, docile and faithful; since the attitudes which underlay them were indistinguishable from his own. One presumes, also, that he would have tried to make clear how in *Gone With the Wind*, the Southerner's long quarrel with Mrs. Stowe eventuated at last in a fiction as moving and memorable as *Uncle Tom's Cabin* itself.

Though no character in his novels, or any of the anti-

Tom books which preceded it, has passed into the mythology of the mass audience, Scarlett, Melanie, Rhett Butler, Ashley Wilkes and Mammy live on in the popular imagination as vividly as Uncle Tom, Eliza, Topsy, Simon Legree and Little Eva. All but one of Miss Mitchell's mythic characters, however, are white. And though the Black Rapist, the archetypal "Bad Nigger," foreshadowed in Dixon and Griffith's Gus, makes a brief appearance in her pages, he has proved less memorable than her "Good Niggers," who serve, protect and, as Faulkner liked to put it, "endure." When all else of the Old South is gone with the wind: the armies of the Confederacy defeated, the great houses pillaged and burned, the courtly lovers—whether impotent cavaliers like Ashley Wilkes or sexy scoundrels like Rhett Butler—departed, her Good Nigger-in-chief, "Mammy" still remains to preside over the book's bittersweet ending.

Like all protagonists of the domestic counter-tradition in American letters, Scarlett O'Hara must be last seen "going home," rather than fleeing to the wilderness, like the anti-domestic Huckleberry Finn. But who is left to welcome her back? Her always shadowy aristocratic mother has long since disappeared, followed by her Irish immigrant father, who has first gone mad; and her children, in whom the childless Margaret Mitchell has never been able to make us quite believe, have died or mysteriously vanished from the scene. Only "Mammy" remains, as she must, since "home" is where she has always been, will always be. "And Mammy will be there," Scarlett re-assures herself.

Certainly she is there in the book's final paragraph, in which Scarlett prepares to return to Tara: "Suddenly she wanted Mammy desperately, as she had wanted her when she was a little girl, wanted the broad bosom, on which to lay her head, the gnarled black hand on her hair. Mammy, the last link with the old days." But "Mammy," we realize at this point, whom no betrayal can alienate, no Emancipation Proclamation force from the eternal bondage of love, is really Uncle Tom, the Great Black Mother of us all.

Even before *Gone With the Wind*, his/her true sex had been revealed: in Faulkner's Dilsey, for instance, whose epitaph (in the androgynous plural) closes *The Sound and the Fury*, "DILSEY. They endured."; and in Aunt Jemima, whose turbaned head has grinned at three generations of Americans from the pancake box that is her final home. But it took Margaret Mitchell, that 1920's flapper and newspaper sob-sister turned laureate to a nation by the Great Depression, to fix her new image for all time. The other women we remember out of this essentially feminine book, from honey-dripping Melanie to mindless, heartless Scarlett, are projections of the author, when they are not stock-figures, like Belle Watling, the Whore with a Heart of Gold. But Mammy she inherits from the book she thought she despised, the dream of a love transcending the horrors of slavery, first dreamed for the Mothers of America by Harriet Beecher Stowe.

Indeed, almost all of Margaret Mitchell's "darkies," as she preferred to call them, seem latter-day versions of Mrs. Stowe's incredibly faithful and naive hero/heroine; since she perceives them through the same haze of genteel, "female" sensibility as her "abolitionist" predecessor. "Negroes," she instructs us, speaking for herself and Scarlett, "had to be handled gently, as though they were children, directed, praised, petted, scolded..." And, she would have us believe, they *were* so treated in the antebellum South, whatever readers of *Uncle Tom's Cabin* may have been misled into thinking was the case. It is, in fact, with such readers that she is quarreling, rather than with the book itself (which, indeed, she may never have read) in the single passage in which she mentions it by name. "Accepting *Uncle Tom's Cabin* as revelation," she writes, "second only to the Bible, the Yankee women all wanted to know about the bloodhounds which every Southerner kept to track down runaway slaves... They wanted to know about the dreadful branding irons which the planters used to mark the faces of their slaves and the cat-o'-nine-tails with which they beat them to death and they evidenced what Scarlett felt was a very nasty and ill-bred interest in slave concubinage..."

She seems never quite to have realized how much the fate of her own book was to be like that of Mrs. Stowe's, its acceptance by the majority audience as a new, revised secular scripture leading to its rejection by literary critics. From the moment of publication, it was faulted, especially in quarters where a taste for High Literature was combined with leftist politics, for its exploitation of "false sentiment and heady goo," along with its promulgation of the presumably defunct "plantation legend." To such attacks, Miss Mitchell purported to be indifferent, "I'd have to do so much explaining to family and friends," she wrote, "if the aesthetes and radicals of literature liked it"—adding in an apology which seems to echo that of Mrs. Stowe. "I'm not a stylist, God knows, and couldn't be if I tried..." Yet something in her seems to have yearned for critical acclaim, so that she responded immediately and gratefully to the favorable notices in the more popular reviews.

For a little while, in fact, the issue seemed in doubt, but once a best-selling movie had been made of *Gone With the Wind*, she was doomed to critical oblivion, especially since the film proved to be as aesthetically undistinguished as her prose. Though credited to a single director and scriptwriter, it was actually directed by two and written by eleven or twelve, a patchwork job with no controlling intelligence behind it, except her own. The millions who first read, then saw *Gone With the Wind* responded to it not as literature but as myth; remembering not even the original author, much less those responsible for adapting her novel to the screen, but the actors who embodied her *personae*: Clark Gable, already mythic before he was cast as Rhett, and Vivien Leigh, who became mythic from the moment she became Scarlett.

To most of those millions, ignorant or indifferent to history, the Defeat of the Confederacy and the Burning of Atlanta, represented a legend not of the ante-bellum past but the mid-Depression present. Though she had begun her novel in the 'twenties, Miss Mitchell finished it under the shadow of the great collapse of 1929; and as she revised it for publication, unemployment, strikes and the threat of violence possessed the streets of our desolate cities; while overseas Nazis and Communists goosestepped and chanted, evoking the menace of conquest and war. Small wonder then that it became the most popular work of the age.

Yet no history of our literature in the 'thirties, written then or since, considers it worthy of mention side by side with the novels of James T. Farrell, John Dos Passos, John Steinbeck, Nathanael West or Henry Roth. Dismissed contemptuously to the underworld of best-sellerdom, it is recalled, if at all, as evidence of the decline of taste in an age of Mass Culture. In Gershom Legman's *Love and Death*, for instance, a hysterical attack on comic-books and best-sellers which appeared in 1948, it is condemned, along with such forgotten pot-boilers as *Forever Amber* and *Duchess Hotspur*, as one more debased celebration of the "Bitch Heroine." "The message..." Legman cries out in righteous indignation, "is hate. Nothing more. Hate, and the war between the sexes, set, symbolically enough—... to the tune of *That's Why the Ku Klux Klan Was Born*."

In an important sense, Gershom Legman is right. *Gone With the Wind* is as much a sado-masochistic work as *Uncle Tom's Cabin*, *The Clansman*, *The Birth of a Nation* and *Roots*, for like them, it is based on a fantasy of inter-ethnic rape as the supreme expression of the violence between sexes and races. In the continuing underground epic of which it is a part, it scarcely matters whether white men are shown sexually exploiting Black Girls or Black men murderously assaulting white ones; only that the male rapist be represented as unmitigatedly evil and the female victim as utterly innocent. This simplistic feminist mythology, Margaret Mitchell qualifies somewhat by making her White female more predatory bitch than passive and helpless sufferer. Nonetheless, it is only the White Woman she is able to imagine threatened; even her passing reference to "slave concubinage," as we have seen, avoiding the mythologically loaded word "rape."

Of the three attempted rapes of Scarlett which dominate the book, however, a Black Man is involved in only one; and even in that instance, he is provided with a rather ineffectual white accomplice. The other two rapists, the first foiled by Scarlett herself, and the second successful because in some sense she collaborates

64

in her violation, are mythological threats to the Southern lady of quite different kinds: the first, a Union Soldier, and the second, a Husband. Both scenes, however, end in the counter-climax of death; the latter stirring in us pity as well as terror; the former terror mitigated only by self-righteous satisfaction, as Scarlett shoots in the face at point-blank range the Union Soldier who dares assault her in her own home. Miss Mitchell takes great pains to make the scene as effective as it is central: "All alone, little lady?" the blue-coated invader asks suggestively, and before she or the reader quite knows what is happening, it is all over. " ... Scarlett ran down the stairs and stood ... gazing down into what was left of the face ... a bloody pit where the nose had been, glazing eyes burned with powder ... " That scene was equally well rendered in the movie version, so well rendered, in fact, that the first-night audience in Miss Mitchell's native Atlanta rose to its feet and cheered.

The second White-White rape, however, that of Scarlett by Rhett Butler, elicited more tears than cheers, when it eventuated in an aborted pregnancy on the great staircase which the film made as mythological as those protagonists themselves. First, however, Scarlett achieves in the arms of Rhett, her husband still though long since banned from her bed, what is apparently the only orgasm of her life, unless she had earlier achieved one blowing the head off the Yankee soldier. (Miss Mitchell is so cagey about such matters that it is hard to be sure.) Nonetheless, this time, too, death is the fruit of love, as Rhett forces her to stumble on the same stairs where he began the assault, and she loses the child she has conceived in his brutal but satisfactory embrace.

Only in a third encounter, occurring midway between the other two, is the would-be-rapist what Dixon had taught Miss Mitchell was the proper mythological color. And it remains, therefore, an archetypal scene, however undercut by the author's insistence that Scarlett may have provoked the attempt at rape, deliverately or foolishly. For a moment, Miss Mitchell seems on the verge of suggesting, in fact, that *all* such outrages arise not out of the lustful obsession with white female flesh that presumably afflicts all Black men, but in part at least out of the troubled erotic dreams (cued half by fear, half by wish) of Southern White women. In the end, however, the language and tone Miss Mitchell uses in describing the attack are scarcely distinguishable from those of Dixon, as in a kind of nightmare transformation her faithful Negro retainer, Big Sam, turns into a Black Rapist: "The negro was beside her, so close that she could smell the rank odor of him...she felt his big hand at her throat and, with a ripping noise, her basque was torn open from neck to waist. Then the black hand fumbled between her breasts and terror and revulsion... came over her and she screamed like an insane woman." This time, too, Big Sam has been no more successful in his attempt at righteous murder than was Scarlett; so that the final act of revenge is left, as is proper to the anti-Tom tradition, to the white riders of the Ku Klux Klan.

It is, however, not her penchant for violence which has kept Margaret Mitchell from critical recognition. To many pious opponents of violence in the arts, her sadism remains as invisible as it apparently was to her, camouflaged by what they take to be her "good intentions." They remember not the terror which moves them below the level of full consciousness, but the heroism of Scarlett, and especially the high romance of her troubled relationship with Rhett Butler. The single line, for instance, that most readers and viewers of *Gone With the Wind*

66

can quote is the one Rhett speaks as he leaves her, perhaps forever, "My dear, I don't give a damn." For elite critics, on the other hand, whom the s-m overtones of Hemingway do not trouble at all (as they did, in fact, trouble Miss Mitchell), the low piety and high romance of her novel aggravate rather than mitigate its violence.

What they cannot finally forgive her is her failure to redeem melodrama with high style and pretentious philosophizing, her giving away of the secret they try so desperately to keep: the fact that *all* literature which long endures and pleases many does so largely by providing the vulgar satisfactions of horror, sexual titillation and the release to tears. This is why *The Literary History of the United States*, for example, devotes not a single line of all of its fourteen hundred odd pages to a discussion of *Gone With the Wind* as literature, merely reporting the statistics of its sales at home and abroad, as if it were an event in the market place and not the Republic of Letters.

For similar reasons, I long concealed my own real affection for the novel and the movie, not only from those whom I addressed in my critical books but from myself. A year or two ago, however, a letter arrived on my desk, addressed to "Dr. Lesley Fielder"—spelling both my names wrong and thus setting into operation habits of condescension, which at that point I had learned to be ashamed of but not to repress. "Dear Lesley Fielder," it began, "It is my understanding and that of my A.P. English Class at Sacred Heart Academy [here once more, triggering automatic condescension] that you feel there are no great female characters in American Literature. I feel, however, that Scarlett O'Hara of Margaret Mitchell's *Gone With the Wind* should be considered etc. etc." And it concluded, "I am writing to you because of your literary background and I would like to know your opinion of my opinion..."

When I still had proper literary opinions, still thought I knew what "literature" was, I would have written (and, indeed, found myself at the point of writing): "My dear So and So, My generalization about there being no great female characters in American Literature still stands, since *Gone With the Wind* is not really a part of American Literature, but only of sub- or para-literature." And I was on the point of referring my correspondent back to *Love and Death in the American Novel*, in which I had dealt with that novel (nearly twenty years before) in a passage full of phrases like "popular literature... fat traditional book...stereotypes...sentimentality... best-seller... ready-made masturbatory fantasies..."

It occurred to me, however, that not only had I come to believe that the lonely act of reading had always and inevitably something masturbatory about it (and, in any case, who *cared*?) but that citing just those words would not have told the whole truth about my attitudes toward that book even way back in 1960. I had, after all, devoted to it two full pages of the six hundred I had allotted myself to cover the whole span of our fiction. And how could I not, having been haunted then, as—like almost all Americans—I continue to be to this day, by scenes, characters, images, names grown mythological, out of that despised novel. Why, then, I found myself pondering over that still unanswered letter, had I so long resisted really coming to terms with the appeal of *Gone With the Wind*, and, indeed, with all other books like it which constitute Popular Literature, Mass Literature, Majority Literature, as opposed to High Literature, Belles Lettres, the "Classics."

Clearly, I have been exposed for many years in classes in English to a kind of systematic brainwashing, in the course of which I learned first to despise and then to sport my contempt for all fiction the enjoyment of which joins me to rather than separates me from "ordinary readers," which is to say, from those of my family and friends who have not made it all the way to a Ph.D. in Literature, but who have stopped short with an M.A., a B.A. or a high-school diploma.

Moreover, I discover that even now, despite my commitment to a populist aesthetics, I am not completely free of ambivalence on this score: an ambivalence reflected in the vestigial scorn I cannot quite repress for the girl from Sacred Heart Academy who begins with a high regard for *Gone With the Wind* rather than *ends* with it (like me) after having passed through an initiation into the world of elitist standards. Precisely because of that initiation, there persists in me a sneaky inclination to believe that Scarlett O'Hara, despite the mythic dimensions she has achieved over the past forty years, does not deserve to be mentioned in the same breath with other archetypal figures out of our literature, like Natty Bumppo, Captain Ahab, Daisy Miller or Hester Prynne, much less their European prototypes like Odysseus, Aeneas, Hamlet, Don Quixote, Medea, Jocasta or Emma Bovary.

Yet I would be hard-pressed to defend such hierarchical distinctions, which depend on what I am convinced is a definition of literature no longer viable in a mass society. And I am willing to follow wherever the logic of my anti-elitist position takes me, even if this means the redemption not just of works I have always, however secretly, loved, *Gone With the Wind, The Birth of a Nation, Uncle Tom's Cabin* but even of such

69

a prefabricated piece of commodity literature as Alex Haley's *Roots*, subsidized by *Readers Digest* and blessed by the *P.T.A.* and, therefore evoking in me an initial distrust I find it harder to overcome.

5 Anti-Anti-Tom Novels and the Decline of the American Empire: Alex Haley's *Roots*

Alex Haley's best-selling novel is in many ways an equivocal, even a duplicitous book, and it is still too early to tell whether it will outlive its immediate popularity. But its importance cannot be denied; for with *Roots*, a Black American succeeded for the first time in modifying the mythology of Black-White relations *for the majority audience*. Other Black American writers of considerable talent have attempted to re-mythologize themselves and their people from the time of Jean Toomer to that of Ishmael Reed.

They have moved, however, not the masses, Black or White, but an elite of professional readers, chiefly White, on whose guilt, self-hatred and self-righteousness they battened. Even Richard Wright, whose *Native Son* became a play and a movie, never managed to capture the great audience; so that the name of his protagonist, "Bigger Thomas," remains completely unknown to the millions of television viewers to whom Scarlett O'Hara's "Mammy" and Haley's "Kunta Kinte" are familiar household names.

It is the nature of our disreputable epic tradition that its laureates are drawn from groups peripheral in a culture controlled by White Anglo-Saxon Protestant

Males: chiefly so far, as we have seen, women and Scotch-Irish "crackers." One of the advantages, in fact, of abandoning the traditional standards of High Culture is that it makes possible the recognition of works by such authors, which tend to be aesthetically naive or marginally literate. In light of all this, it was inevitable that sooner or later a Black American hack writer would become one of the makers of our Communal Dream. What could not have been predicted, however, is that his book when finally published would not only, like Mrs. Stowe's, be "read equally in the parlor, the kitchen and the nursery," but be condensed in the *Readers Digest* and assigned in every classroom in the land.

Indeed, the almost universal acclaim accorded *Roots* makes it different from earlier contributions to our inadvertent epic. *Uncle Tom's Cabin* finally divided readers, politically and geographically, right down the middle; so that pro-Slavery Southerners had to read it secretly, if at all. And sophisticated Black readers continue, to this day, the quarrel with her insidiously seductive myth. In 1976, for instance, the year in which *Roots* appeared, Ishmael Reed, a favorite of elitist critics, published a novel called *Flight to Canada*, the preface to which is a bitter attack on Mrs. Stowe as a snob and plagiarist:

Old Harriet. Naughty Harriet. Accusing Lord Byron of pornography. She couldn't take to Lincoln. She liked Nobility. Curious. The woman who was credited with ruining the Planters was a toady to Nobility, just as they were. Strange, history. Complicated, too. It will always be a mystery, history. New disclosures are as bizarre as the most bizarre fantasy.

Harriet caught some of it. She popularized the American

novel and introduced it to Europe. *Uncle Tom's Cabin*. Writing is strange, though. That story caught up with her. The story she "borrowed" from Josiah Henson. Harriet only wanted enough money to buy a silk dress. The paper mills ground day and night. She'd read Josiah Henson's book. That Harriet was alert. *The Life of Josiah Henson, Formerly a Slave*. Seventy-seven pages long. It was short, but it was his. It was all he had. His story.

The anti-Tom books which responded to Mrs. Stowe's proved equally controversial, since they too subverted the reigning values of the age in which they appeared. Dixon is remembered as a rabid racist; *The Birth of a Nation* is banned in some quarters even now; and Margaret Mitchell, scorned by the left-wing intellectuals of her own time, was still being evoked as the ultimate Enemy by the Black Nationalists of the 'sixties. Malcolm X, for instance, recalling his youth, writes: "I remember one thing that marred this time for me: the movie 'Gone With the Wind.' When it played in Mason, I was the only Negro in the theater, and when Butterfly MacQueen went into her act, I felt like crawling under the rug."

But the only voices raised against *Roots* were those of a few hysterical rightists, discredited in the eyes of establishment liberals and conservatives alike, even before the appearance of their scarcely literate Letters to the Editor. Ishmael Reed, it is true, has made some disparaging remarks about Haley's best-seller; but his reservations are clearly cued by the fact that it not merely outsold but obliterated his own book.

Most other defenders of High Literature in dealing with a book as awkwardly structured and ineptly written as *The Clansman* itself, salved their consciences with a few apologetic reservations or retreated into abashed silence; when they did not, like James Baldwin, tout it extravagantly. "An act of faith and courage..." he wrote of *Roots*, "an act of love...it suggests with great power how each of us...can't but be the vehicle of the history which produced us." He had apparently forgotten at that point the lesson taught him by Richard Wright, and recorded in his essay, "Alas, Poor Richard": "'Roots,' Richard would snort, when I had finally worked my way around to this dreary subject, 'what—roots! Next thing you'll be telling me is that all colored folks have rhythm.'"

Nor did he apparently remember that he had condemned Mrs. Stowe for precisely the combination of sentimentality and brutality which constitutes the essential appeal of Haley's novel. A reader unfamiliar with *Gone With the Wind* would have a hard time telling Margaret Mitchell's ironic précis of *Uncle Tom's Cabin* ("... the bloodhounds which every Southerner kept to track down runaway slaves...the dreadful branding irons which planters used to mark...their slaves and the cat-o'-nine-tails with which they beat them to death... slave concubinage...") from a plot-summary of what happens to Haley's Kunta Kinte after falling into the hands of White Slavers.

Yet Mrs. Stowe's name is never mentioned by Alex Haley. Indeed, *Roots* may well be the only notable book written by a Black American which contains not a single reference to *Uncle Tom's Cabin*. Even the terms "Tom" and "Uncle Tom," are oddly absent; though Haley's most eminent Afro-American predecessors use those epithets as often and as automatically as black street people, who may not even know the name of Mrs. Stowe. Such writers, moreover, never fail to mention her book, against which they strive to define themselves in desperate ambivalence. That Richard Wright called the anti-Tom hero of *Native Son* "Bigger Thomas" in due deliberation is attested to by the fact that he entitled his first collection of stories *Uncle Tom's Chillun*, and James Baldwin, his self-declared spiritual "heir," carries on the tradition. Even in the iconoclastic 'sixties, Malcolm X takes time out from tirades against the White "Devils" to inform us that "Of course, I read *Uncle Tom's Cabin*. In fact, I believe that's the only novel I have ever read since I started serious reading"; and Eldridge Cleaver interrupts his meditations on black and white sexuality in *Soul on Ice* to observe that "The most alienated view of America was preached by...Harriet Beecher Stowe in Uncle Tom's Cabin."

All of them, however, end by rejecting her androgynous Christian protagonist as a role model, identifying instead with the prepotent "Bad Nigger," the rapist of White women, first projected in fear and loathing by Dixon, Griffith and Margaret Mitchell, and re-embodied in Wright's "Bigger." "No American Negro exists," James Baldwin once remarked, "who does not have his private Bigger Thomas living in the skull." But the inarticulate and apolitical Bigger was, we remember, the improbable alter ego of a super-articulate Communist author, married to a White woman; and perhaps for this reason, Wright could not *quite* manage to make him perform the archetypal act of darkness. It is a Black Girl whom Bigger actually rapes and murders, after having lusted for but not assaulted, then half-accidentally killed a white one. To be sure, he hacks off her head, providing an atrocity bloody enough to satisfy guilty white liberals and angry Blacks; but he remains, all the same, a kind of crypto-Good-Bad Nigger.

Not until the triumph and collapse of the Civil Rights

Movement, in which Black and White males had stood shoulder to shoulder in a relationship presided over by the Myth of Huck and Jim on the Raft, was the Dixonian myth of the Bad Nigger fully introjected by American Blacks. "Come up, black dada nihilismus," LeRoi Jones chanted in *The Dead Lecturer*. "Rape the white girls. Rape their fathers. Cut the mothers' throats." And Eldridge Cleaver first lived, then translated back into literature in *Soul on Ice* the nightmare role of the revolutionary Black Rapist: "I became a rapist...I started out by practising on black girls in the ghetto...and when I considered myself smooth enough, I crossed the tracks and sought out white prey...Rape was an insurrectionary act."

The moment which produced such manifestos, however, is ten years past; and though the Black pride it nurtured survives, it has shed the abrasive militancy and intransigent separatism of the late 'sixties. It demands, therefore, myths not of Black brutalization debouching in murder and rape, but of the persistence in the Black community of dignity, heroism, along with such bourgeois virtues as piety, domesticity and sexual fidelity. Descriptions of the "essential blackness" of Black life in white America, therefore, like the classic passage in Richard Wright's *Black Boy* ("...I used to mull over the strange absence of real kindness in Negroes, how unstable was our tenderness, how lacking in genuine passion we were, how void of great hope, how timid our joy, how bare our traditions, how hollow our memories, how lacking we were in those intangible sentiments which bind man to man...") have come to seem irrelevant, offensive, untrue.

In some ways, Mrs. Stowe's idyllic legend of Black

family life under slavery is more like what our age demands; but to sustain this myth of the Black Family in the late 'seventies a new myth of Africa is required, and here she proves of little use. Her genteel, feminist dream of Mother Africa beating the patriarchal swords of Anglosaxondom into ploughshares has come, indeed, to seem as quaint as Edgar Rice Burroughs' *macho* nightmare of a Dark Continent of predators and cannibals responsive only to force. Neither is the Mau Mau model of counter-terror, so dear to the hearts of the early Black Panthers, entirely satisfactory, any more than the dream dreamed by the Harlem Renaissance of Africa as the Black Man's "unspeakably, dark, guilty, erotic past," driven underground by White Puritanism. What has been revived in their place is the Romantic myth of the Noble Savage, as translated in the Afro-American Cultural centers of the United States, where dark-skinned young men and women in quest of a tradition learn Swahili, dress in dashikis and dance to jungle drums.

The image that possesses them is no longer that of the "Good Good Nigger" as projected in Uncle Tom, or of the "Bad Bad Nigger" as embodied in Eldridge Cleaver—but of the "Good Bad Nigger" as imagined by Malcolm X *after* his break with Elijah Mohammed. Malcolm X, however, dead at the hands of fellow Blacks, did not survive to write the scriptures of the new mythology. And, in any case, he was not a writer of books, only a maker of speeches and a scribbler of cryptic notes on crumpled napkins, from which his so-called "autobiography" was re-constructed by Alex Haley, a writer of fiction, who had to believe for reasons of his own that he was dealing with fact. A regular contributor to the *Readers Digest*, his model not just for

The Autobiography of Malcolm X but for Roots as well, was that standard *Digest* piece, "The Most Unforgettable Character I Have Ever Known."

It is indeed his ability to make it at the heart of the White Establishment, for twenty years in the Coast Guard, and for ten more in the mass media, which qualified Haley to become the laureate of Black-White relations in a time of accommodation. He is, in short, a Good Good Nigger, an "Uncle Tom," late twentieth-century style. At least that is what he seemed in Malcolm X's eyes—and reflexively in his own—at the moment of their first meeting. No wonder, then, that the epithet he avoided in *Roots*, appears in Haley's description of that meeting. "We got off to a very poor start," Haley explains. "To use a word he liked, I think both of us were a bit 'spooky'...I had heard him bitterly attack other Negro writers as 'Uncle Toms'... My twenty years in the military service and my Christian religious persuasion didn't help either..."

Earlier in the book, Haley had reported Malcolm X as saying, "Today's Uncle Tom doesn't wear a handkerchief on his head... He's usually well-dressed and well educated...a professional Negro..." Yet Haley cannot resist reporting the "professional" qualifications of his own family in his book's final "Happy Ending." Strategically suppressed by the White script writers of the TV version of *Roots*, it is confessed in the backjacket blurb of the paper-back edition, which boasts that his saga "ends...at the Arkansas funeral of a Black professor whose children are a teacher, a Navy architect, an assistant director of the U.S. Information Agency, and an author. The author is Alex Haley."

And this seems fair enough in light of the fact that,

throughout the book, Haley strives to portray his fore-
bears even in Africa aspiring to a bourgeois life-style
that would have pleased Mrs. Stowe. When Chicken
George, for instance, prophesies, for the benefit of his
wife, Matilda, the domestic Utopia which lies ahead for
them after freedom, he does so in the following terms:
"How you reckon you look settin' in yo' own house, yo'
own stuffed furniture, an' all dem knicknacks? How
'bout Miss Tilda axin' de other free nigger womens over
for tea in de mornin's, an y'all jes' settin' 'roun talkin'
'bout 'rangin' y'all's flowers, an sich as dat?''

It is, however, not that simple; since finally *Roots* is
not really a Tom-Book, anymore than it is an anti-Tom
one. It is an anti-anti-Tom book; its most memorable,
which is to say, its only truly mythic character, Kunta
Kinte, an anti-anti Tom: an unreconstructed Noble
African, who after a symbolic castration and a Happy
Marriage becomes a Good Bad Nigger, passing on the
hope of freedom but running away no more. In light of
this, it scarcely matters how true to scholarship or the
living Africans' perception of their own past Haley's
version of Kunta Kinte is. Anthropologists have
charged that he was taken in by a notably unreliable
Griot or Oral Historian; and the Gambian government
two years after he had released his first findings barred
all Afro-Americans from becoming permanent resi-
dents in their country. But the book continues to move
millions of readers, unaware that Kunta Kinte is less a
portrait of Haley's first American ancestor, legendary or
real, than of Malcolm X as Haley perceived him in guilt
or envy.

Even as the living Haley ghost-wrote the *Autobiography*, Malcolm X, from beyond the grave, ghost-
wrote what is most authentic and moving in *Roots*—

the story of Kunta Kinte. Like Malcolm X, the Moslem Kunta Kinte rejects his White Christian name; dreams of a return to Africa not just for himself but for all Black Americans; is an old-fashioned Sexist, believing that women should not be taught to read and that their place is in the Home; and an inverted Racist, convinced that all Whites not only invariably do evil to all Blacks, but that they have an offensive odor, and are properly classified not as human but as *toubob*, "devils" who must be resisted unto death. Like the almost-White Black Moslem who possessed him, Haley is driven to euphemize Africa, even as he vilifies the American South. Though he perfunctorily admits the existence of slavery on that continent and the complicity of Black Americans in the Slave trade, he manages to make them seems innocuous, even as he does the prevailing violence of African life. If someone is forever beating someone else in Haley's Gambian village, it is *for their own good*; only White men presumably being capable of gratuitous brutality.

It is, however, in the area of sexuality that Haley most flagrantly falsifies the record. Though his Mandinkas are Moslems committed to polygamy, Haley cannot bring himself to portray Kunta Kinte's father as having taken a second wife. And though tribal custom demands that men do not marry until they are thirty and thirty-five, he would have us believe that there was no pre-marital sex among the Mandinkas; so that Kunta Kinte (in the book's most palpable absurdity) remains a virgin until he is 39! Haley may have been influenced in this by the twelve year celibacy which Malcolm X imposed on himself from the moment he became a Moslem until the time he discovered that his spiritual leader, Elijah Mohammed was sexually exploiting his female secretaries. But finally his sexual reticence (like his squeamish insistence that all black slave children wore diapers) tells us more about Haley and his commitment to monogamy and bourgeois values than it does about Malcolm X.

Sexual passion in *Roots* (except for the comic Porgy and Bess tomcatting of Chicken George) is portrayed as essentially evil: the final indignity visited by White Male Masters on Black Female Slaves, even as whipping is inflicted by those same masters on Black males—often their own children. Scenes of rape and flagellation are as essential to his vision as to that of Mrs. Stowe or Thomas Dixon, Jr. or Margaret Mitchell; though his victims are, of course, always Black. Nowhere is there any hint that Black Men may even desire, much less violate White Women; nor even any suggestion that Black girls may have, on occasion, invited, welcomed or boasted about being chosen as bed-partners of "Old Massa." This is left for high-brow ironists like Ishmael Reed, more interested in subverting the stereotypes of the mass audience, Black or White, than in exploiting them pruriently.

Whatever his motives, Haley ends by providing his audience (chiefly White, it would seem, at least as far as print is concerned; since less than one percent of the letters he got in response to the condensed *Digest* version came from Blacks) with the double pleasure of vicariously indulging in inter-ethnic rape or flagellation then indignantly deploring them. The purplest passage in *Roots*—rendered in even greater detail than the beatings or brandings—is the description of the rape of Kizzy by Massa Tom Lea: "As she flailed her arms in agony and arched her back to shake him off, he banged her head against the floor, again, again, again, then began slapping her—more and more excitedly—until Kizzy felt her dress being snatched upward, her undergarments being ripped . . . she felt his hands fumbling upward between her thighs, finding, fingering her private parts, squeezing and spreading them . . . Then came the searing pain as he forced his way into her . . .''

This is, of course, not documented history, but, like three quarters of Haley's book, fiction: based in this case, on a fantasy as endemic in the collective unconscious of America as the rape and murder of White innocence at the hands of Black lust. It is also the portrait of a male ancestor, two generations closer to Arthur Haley than the African Kunta Kinte; yet we are not permitted in this scene to think of ''roots,'' since Massa Lea is White and therefore does not mythically count as an ancestor, only as a source of ''pollution,'' as Haley had learned from listening to Malcolm X.

How pointless, then, the debate about the historical veracity of Haley's genealogy, except insofar as it reminds us that *all* contributions to our inadvertent prose epic have claimed to be more truth than fantasy—and were in that sense ''hoaxes.'' Not just the works of Mrs. Stowe and Dixon, D. W. Griffith and Margaret Mitchell, but the Slave Narratives and White histories of Reconstruction on which they drew were, to one degree or another, fictional constructs.

The relation of *Uncle Tom's Cabin* to the Slave Narrative of Josiah Henson is especially interesting in this regard. Ishmael Reed is wrong. Only after she wrote her best-seller, did Mrs. Stowe discover it, citing it to prove to her pro-slavery opponents that Good Good Niggers did in fact exist. But Henson, it turns out, was not that good after all; and in any case his "true" account had been ghost-written by a White journalist, who was not above amending it in later editions to make it conform even more closely to Mrs. Stowe's novel. Henson himself, though cagey at first, ended by claiming, perhaps even believing, that he was the original authentic Uncle Tom. And Mrs. Stowe came to believe it, too, collaborating with Henson in inventing a meeting between them which seems never to have occurred. The surfiction or meta-myth which they thus created has ever since been exploited for the benefit of American tourists by the Chamber of Commerce of the small Ontario town in which Henson died, even as the airline which organizes tours to Gambia exploits Haley's mytho-history of his family.

There are indeed some members of Haley's audience, ashamed of the rootlessness which was once the American's proudest boast, for whom *Roots* does not function as fiction at all; representing not one more myth of race and sex in America, but the replacement of all such myths by the unchangeable, irrefutable truth. If, however, Haley's *Roots* is to survive a definition of "truth" dependent on shifting pieties of the moment, this will be because it responds to less transient-buried beliefs. Most of these pieties, I must confess, I do not share. I believe as little, for instance, in the absolute purity (or malevolence) of all native Africans, as I do in the unmitigated malevolence (or purity) of all Southern White Americans; and I remain indifferent to the claims of genealogists, quite content to think of my remotest ancestors as, thank god, myths. Yet much of Haley's *Roots* moves me deeply.

Like *The Clansman* and *The Leopard's Spots*—indeed, like all majority literature—it stirs wonder in us by evoking primordial images, sentimental, violent, prurient, of necessity, *gross*. Works which long endure win our assent not rationally and logically, like history, philosophy or science, but viscerally, passionately, like rituals in primitive societies or dreams in our own. They tend, that is to say, to reinforce our wildest paranoid delusions, along with our most utopian hopes about the relations of races, sexes and generations: self-indulgent reveries, from which we rouse ourselves in embarrassment, or nightmares from which we wake in terror—but which continue to resonate in our waking heads, whether we be racists, chauvinists, fascists and practising sadists, or rightminded liberals, pacifists, feminists and twice-born Christians.

It is, indeed, the function of all art at its most authentic to release us to dionysiac, demonic impulses; and thus to satisfy our shame-faced longing (otherwise repressed or sublimated) to be driven out of control—to permit us, in short, moments of privileged madness, a temporary return to psychic states which we have theoretically abandoned in the name of humanity and sweet reason.

Quite obviously, not only sophisticated artists can produce such works, skilled craftsmen who have lived exemplary lives and worked hard at their trade. They are in the power of anyone—good or evil, energetic or indolent, intelligent or stupid, who is gifted with easy access to his own unconscious and to the collective fantasies of his time and place. Once we have understood this, we will know why the most important, beloved and moving books do not have to pass the traditional tests we pedagogue-critics have imposed on literature in the name of the Aristotelian formula "instruct and delight."

To impart wisdom or to make elegant structures, to console and uplift the heart are optional for song and story—not forbidden, but not required either. What is required is to stir wonder and ecstacy, thus enabling us to be "in dreams awake." Once we have realized this, we will have begun to define a new way of evaluating such long-underesteemed writers as Stowe and Mitchell and Dixon and Haley, inept in form and weak in ideas, but like Shakespeare or Sophocles, Dickens or Mark Twain, endowed—by the grace of God, the muse of their own unconscious—with mythopoeic power.